"Brilliant! I want to read it over and over, slowly, and deliberately, savoring every word. McGee Baird and Coughlin demonstrate how, with deliberate intention, we can build a program worthy of our children, our families, our teams, and ourselves. Through story sharing and clear achievable steps, they invite us to think about how we can create space for reflection, and build our environments through respect, trust, and collaboration. A must read for all lead positions within child care organizations and for those aspiring to be leads. This is how I want to live and work."

—Sheila Olan-Maclean, CEO, Compass Early Learning & Care

"An inspiring and insightful resource. Finally, a book that will become my pedagogical companion! *Creating a Culture of Reflective Practice* will be referred to time and time again by educators and pedagogical leaders that would like to reflect and grow their practice."

—Paola Hohenadel, RECE, MEd, Affiliated Services for Children and Youth (ASCY), Hamilton, Ontario

"As an organization committed to pedagogy, we have had the pleasure firsthand to experience the work of Lorrie and Anne Marie and believe them to be 'drivers' of pedagogy across our Province and nationally. Throughout their book, Lorrie and Anne Marie offer a variety of thought-provoking reflective questions that help shift practice. As a pedagogical leader, offering opened questions along with 'reflection' inspires educators to align their values, beliefs, and learning, while developing a critical understanding of their own practice. This provokes educators to consider their own knowledge, skills, and dispositions to achieve the best outcomes for children. Throughout the book, many stories are shared to support educators on their pedagogical journey."

—Lisa Bellardini, RECE, Director of Learning and Pedagogy & Carrie Horn, RECE, Executive Director Hamilton-Wentworth Catholic Child Care Centres

"When early childhood educators and program leaders choose to step away from pre-planned curricula, we may initially find ourselves without much to hold on to. Simply directing educators to pursue a reflective teaching approach—without providing any supportive guidance or practical tools—is just mean! Intentional pedagogical leadership fills that gap, enabling a reflective and responsive experience for educators, children, and families. From a place of deep experience and empathy, Lorrie and Anne Marie offer us relevant and usable strategies for pedagogical leadership, and a robust framework for upholding reflective practice in our classrooms and schools."

—Sarah Felstiner, operations manager, Epiphany Early Learning Preschool

CREATING A CULTURE OF REFLECTIVE PRACTICE

Creating a Culture of Reflective Practice

THE ROLE OF PEDAGOGICAL LEADERSHIP IN EARLY CHILDHOOD PROGRAMS

Anne Marie Coughlin and Lorrie McGee Baird

Redleaf Press®
www.redleafpress.org
800-423-8309

Published by Redleaf Press
10 Yorkton Court
St. Paul, MN 55117
www.redleafpress.org

First edition 2022
Cover design by Jesse Hughes
Cover photos by Cheryl Casey/stock.adobe.com, KMNPhoto/stock.adobe.com, pressmaster/stock.adobe .com, bnenin/stock.adobe.com, Rawpixel.com/stock.adobe.com, Konstiantyn Zapylaie/stock.adobe. com, fizkes/stock.adobe.com
Interior design by Wendy Holdman
Typeset in Latienne Pro and Acumin Pro
Printed in the United States of America

Library of Congress Cataloging-in-Publication Data

Names: Coughlin, Anne Marie, 1964- author. | Baird, Lorrie McGee, author.
Title: Creating a culture of reflective practice : the role of pedagogical leadership in early childhood / by Anne Marie Coughlin and Lorrie McGee Baird.
Description: First Edition. | St. Paul : Redleaf Press, [2022] | Includes bibliographical references and index. | Summary: "Early childhood professionals and leaders need to reconcile the responsibility between never-ending administrative tasks, ensuring program quality and supporting the growth of others. Creating a Culture of Reflective Practice is a comprehensive practical look at creating systems, structures and protocols for supporting people in large and small organizations, individuals working as mentors, coaches or pedagogical leaders to invite educators into a thinking and learning process about their work"—Provided by publisher.
Identifiers: LCCN 2021021749 (print) | LCCN 2021021750 (ebook) | ISBN 9781605547404 (Paperback : acid-free paper) | ISBN 9781605547411 (ePub)
Subjects: LCSH: Educational leadership. | Early childhood education. | Early childhood teachers. | Child care.
Classification: LCC LB2806 .C684 2022 (print) | LCC LB2806 (ebook) | DDC 371.2/011—dc23
LC record available at https://lccn.loc.gov/2021021749
LC ebook record available at https://lccn.loc.gov/2021021750

Printed on acid-free paper U22-06

Dedication

To our fathers who have left us in body but not in spirit.
Thank you for giving us the gift of stories. We love you.

To our mothers, Catherine Darling and Brenda McGee,
who remain our biggest admirers and think we are smarter than we are.

Table of Contents

Foreword

"Time has a wonderful way of showing us what really matters."
 often attributed to Margaret Peters

It's lunchtime for my group of toddlers, and there is much to do before we can sit down to eat. As we come in from the yard, we need to support the children to take off shoes and put them in the shoe basket, hang coats, change diapers, fill out diaper charts, sit on the potty, and wash hands.

We are encouraging a small group in the entry hall with their shoes, and as usually happens, several children are attracted to climbing the stairway next to us. Finally, my coteacher and I convince everyone to come down from the stairs and get their shoes off and into the basket. She leaves for the classroom with a small group of children while I assure her we will follow right behind.

Then, of course, Malcom decides to dump all the shoes out, and with a big grin, puts the basket over his head. If you have ever spent any time with a group of toddlers, I'm sure you can picture this joyful mayhem.

All the children stop what they are doing and look at Malcom with keen interest. I decide to go with this moment. We all peek at Malcom through the holes in the basket and giggle together. We can see him in there! Then, of course, everyone wants to try so we take a little more time as each child puts the basket on their head. After we've all had a turn to peek through the basket—including me!—everyone happily helps put the shoes back in the basket and we head into the room.

My title in this program is mentor teacher, so my job is to work side by side with my coteachers, offering support for our daily life together as well as for reflective practice and curriculum development. Because of my role as one of the classroom educators, I feel the pressure of how much time this first step in our transition has taken, knowing there is so much left to follow. I know my coworker is expecting me to hurry along so we can get to lunch in a timely manner. And yes, I think she would be worried, along with me, about all the shoe germs that might be lingering in that basket.

But after many, many years of working with children and adults in early childhood programs, I am committed to taking time to pause and marvel with the children about what really matters, including this moment of children's delightful connection with each other around Malcom's lively investigation, even if this takes more time than the schedule suggests. Yes, it matters that we embrace the important caregiving tasks, and it matters that we follow a routine to organize our ways to be together, and it's also important to take time for health and safety measures. Making sure I live up to my responsibility with my coworkers really matters to me too.

I can respond to the pressure and rush through this time, focused on looking at the clock and getting the tasks done. But I have come to see that these unfolding moments are what create the quality of our programs, as they nourish both the children and ourselves. It is in these moments where children learn about themselves, grow relationships, help each other, and bring their curious minds to wonder and learn about the world around us. If I help my coteachers take time to pause and appreciate these moments, it brings more joy to our work and gives us opportunities to see the powerful roles we can play together in children's lives. Experiencing the value of studying these delightful encounters encourages our willingness to give the children a little extra time for the moments. Ensuring that we take time to pause, to observe, to study and appreciate the many moments throughout our days with children is the most powerful and effective professional development we can offer.

I have advocated in all of my professional development work and writing for educators that slowing down to notice and take up these moments is vital to the work. The response usually is "We have so much to do that we don't have time." I personally understand this response, as I have spent many years doing this daily work in a busy classroom. Just getting through a day with a group of young children requires so many different tasks: planning, meeting and talking with families, setup, cleanup, nose wiping, conflict resolution, and so much more. The nature of the work leaves us breathless as we hurry to get it all done. We have to make an intentional commitment to take the time for engaging with these moments.

Policy makers, regulators, and administrators develop standards, assessment tools, rating scales, and checklists that they expect us to spend our time doing. We often are required to attend conferences and workshops, usually getting information from "experts" about techniques and curriculum models that specifically tell us how to use our time, often without reflections on ourselves or what is unfolding with our children. And commercial early childhood companies suggest that we can save time by buying their products, rather than observing our children and taking the time to plan, collect, and invent our own creative invitations for their play and learning.

The reality is that it is impossible to magically create additional time in our workday, but as leaders, mentors, and directors we can think more about how educators spend the time we have. We have the power to decide how we use time in staff meetings, planning curriculum, and completing documentation. We can carve out more time in our organizations and model approaches that support educators to use the time they have to pause and study, to nourish themselves and deepen their relationships with each other and their practices with children. Reimagining the use of time is the key to quality programs for children and adults. How we use our time defines who we are as educators, as a program, as a profession, as a community, and as a world.

The most fruitful way to help educators slow down to take time to see what really matters is having someone to work side by side with us. Someone who encourages us to notice and study children's competencies, to name what we see and value during our daily lives. Someone to offer us different points of view, counter inequity, and challenge us to examine our own bias. Someone who shares professional information, current research, required assessments, and checklists and who supports us to reflect on how we can make these meaningful for our daily work. Someone to help us to think of all the possible ways we can make meaning of what is unfolding, rather than look for a "right" way. Someone who helps us identify the roles we might play in children's lives based on our values and what matters to us, the children, and their families. Someone who respects us and knows that we are reflective thinkers who can research answers to our own questions and make meaningful decisions for our work. Someone who helps us live into our best selves as educators. Someone who helps us see the benefit of taking time to do this work for our own lives as humans. And most important, someone who can help carve out and advocate for the time and how to use it to support us to do this crucial reflective work.

The great news is my brilliant friends and colleagues Lorrie McGee Baird and Anne Marie Coughlin have written this book about being one of these supportive people in an educator's life. It is a complex book, with big ideas for working with educators, inviting us to think through our values, define them for ourselves, and support educators to do the same. The concrete way they have organized the book, using many visionary ideas and practical approaches, helps the book be relatable, manageable, and doable. They offer relevant stories to study, reflecting real children, educators, and pedagogical leaders working together in early childhood programs. They specifically outline worthwhile learning experiences to use with children, educators, mentors, and pedagogical leaders. I haven't counted, but I think there may be more than a hundred provocative questions to take up in various aspects of our work with children, families, and each other.

Lorrie and Anne Marie know that what they suggest in this book are not easy, quick fixes. They tell stories of their own learning journey; from teachers who once followed themes and scripts and rigidly defined strategies to reflective educators who invented ways to question their own practices, leading their organizations with a vision for building structures that create a culture of reflective practice. They report on their willingness to take up difficult, complex issues and tease them apart to find meaningful ways to engage and address them.

They discuss one of the current critical issues white women leaders like myself face—moving away from the white supremacist, European-centered foundation of early education to one that strives to center other cultures and ways of being. This is particularly pertinent for the authors' Canadian context when it comes to Indigenous, First Nations people whose land they acknowledge they occupy. You will hear the ways they approach antibias education, social justice, and equity, admitting that this is what they know now while always asserting they have so much to learn and harm to undo.

Lorrie and Anne Marie have created structures for openness throughout this book. It is a term I learned from my long-ago visionary mentors and professors at Pacific Oaks College, Elizabeth Jones and Elizabeth Prescott. The idea behind this term has resonated with me in all my work with children and adults. It suggests that we need a structure or a shared, defined process that helps us focus together on an idea or a task, an open structure designed to invite many possible ideas and ways of learning and being.

I think of organizing my classroom for children with this idea in mind. There is a structure in how we design and arrange the space to make visible the shared approaches for being together. Yet within this structure, children are invited to bring themselves and their own ideas to explore, invent, and work together in many different ways. This same concept can be applied for the structures we plan for our adult learners. Rather than a checklist, assessment, or model that has specific tasks to complete, a structure for openness might include a protocol with a set of questions or an experience that defines a shared understanding of how we will work together to learn. The intention of the structure is to invite many perspectives with different ways of thinking about and accomplishing the work. These structures can contribute to inclusive, equitable approaches to teacher education, as they invite collaboration with attention and respect for diverse perspectives as central to the work.

The authors share many structures for openness and experiences they have successfully used in their work as pedagogical leaders in two large, multisite programs where they have taken the time to slowly and deliberately build structures that support and sustain cultures of reflective practice. I have visited both programs many times and have been in awe with how their work truly reflects the values, practices, and approaches they offer here.

This book is about using time for what matters. And it will take time to study the ideas in the book, try out some of the structures, and ponder the questions. The book will be useful for educators' daily work with children, as you will be inspired to take up the many provocative questions and want to invite others to study your work with you. It will be inspiring for people working as mentors, coaches, and pedagogical leaders, as there are a multitude of innovative practices for engaging adults in studying their work with children. If you are a director, this book will kindle a desire in you to design budgets, staffing, and administrative supports for the time it requires to do work that truly enhances quality. And if you are an administrator, licensor, curriculum developer, or policy maker, perhaps this book will help you see how impactful it could be to develop accountability systems that have reflective practices as their foundation.

If you find yourself thinking "I can't imagine having time for all of this," I would suggest that you use Anne Marie and Lorrie's book as inspiration. Although they give some examples of their own organizational structures for making time, they don't try to answer the logistical or organizational questions for making more time. Only you can reimagine the use of time in your organization and determine how you will carve out more time for creating a culture of reflective practice. This book will show you concrete and inspirational ways to use your time, and, even more important, illustrate why taking this time for reflection is essential for the vibrancy of our programs, the nourishment of our educators, and the quality of experiences for our children and families. This book can help you answer the question: How will we use the time we have for what really matters?

—Deb Curtis

Acknowledgments

We acknowledge that we are settlers who live, love, and work on the traditional and ancestral lands of the Attawandaran, Anishinaabe, Haudenosaunee and Leni-Lunaape peoples, which include: Chippewa of the Thames First Nation, Oneida Nation of the Thames, Munsee-Delaware Nation (Anne Marie) and the traditional territory of the Anishinaabe Mississauga adjacent to Haudenosaunee Territory, collectively known as the Williams Treaties First Nations, which include: Curve Lake, Hiawatha, Alderville, Scugog Island, Rama, Beausoleil, and Georgina Island First Nations (Lorrie). We offer our deep respect to the elders, knowledge keepers, and all first peoples of Turtle Island as we work toward truth and reconciliation together.

Our deepest gratitude to the many educators and pedagogical leaders who have invited us to journey alongside them in learning. You who have graciously opened your doors, hearts, and minds to us are our inspirers, teachers, collaborators, and think partners. Without you, we could not do our work.

To Deb Curtis, who lovingly tricked us into writing this book with her and then left us on our own to do it. Thank you for your unwavering support and guidance and for pushing us from the nest.

To Margie Carter, for your fierce leadership and advocacy and for helping us to see what loving, relentless mentorship looks like in real life.

To Sheila Olan-McLean, Ian Gibb, Michael Harkins, Charlene Grainger, and Angela Woodburn, for your amazing leadership and vision and for creating places where innovative thinking thrives and relationships are central to our work. We hope you understand the impact you have made on our lives.

To our work families at London Bridge Child Care Services and Compass Early Learning and Care, for your enduring trust and encouragement. For decades you have supported us in our relentless desire to question, experiment, and push boundaries. Thank you for holding us up, enabling our successes, and allowing us to fail with grace.

To our dear friends Wendy Cividanes and Debbie Lebo, for your masterful facilitation and extraordinary empathy and for being our trusted critical friends.

To Tammy Johnson, Rukia Rogers, Brian Silveria, Nadia Jaboneta, Alissa Mwenelupembe, Sarah Felstiner, Kelly Ramsey, Kelly Mathews, Kendra Pelojoaquin, Eliana Elias, and Ijuuma Jordan, for your steadfast work in advancing equity and social justice and for being our teachers.

To all of those whose voices have in some way made it into this book, through story or influence, including: Shawna Alexander, Melissa Atkinson, Kennedy Baird, Kinga Baricz, Tracy Barkman, Christine Barrett, Diana Beaty, Lisa Bellardini, Rachel Blanchette, Anna Boulter, Shelley Brandon, Karen Calligan, Debbie Campbell, Bethany Carter, Dr. Jean Clinton, Renee Coughlin, Norma Curtis, Ashley Daley, Elaine DaSilva, Andrea Dewhurst, Karla Fonseca, Priscilla Gately, Charlene Grainger, Hayley Hamilton, Kathy Harris, Julie Harrison, Jeanette Heino, Sabrina Hemeryck, Mary Hewitt, Angela Hoar, Paola Hohenadel, Vicky Jenkinson, Anna Jennings, Lindsay Jessen, Sherida Johnson, Tammy Johnson, Sonya Kim, Melissa Krobisch, Tabitha Lang, Tanis Lavigne, Courtney Lewis, Jess Lowes, Andrea MacIntosh, Linda Magill, Kirsty Mason, Hanah McFarlane, Dan Meteluch, Tonya Millsap, Judy Mulvihill, Katherine Orgill, Gina Orosz, Anne Pelo, Pat Porter, Charlotte Prince, Lindsay Ross, Maria Saunders, Carrie Snook, Gabriella Solti, Jennifer Son, Lindsay Sparkes, Stephanie Springette, Stacey Stothers, Jenny Thompson, Tina Thompson, Judy Topolniski, Dianne Traynor, Breanna Tully, Claudia Valencia, Joanie Vallinga, Jill Wickins, and Angela Woodburn.

To our editor Melissa York, for patiently guiding us to be better writers, and to the whole team at Redleaf Press, for pulling this project together and trusting that we had something valuable to offer.

To our families, for encouraging us to follow our passion, and for still loving us when we might not be so loveable.

To our children, Kennedy Baird and Renee, Noelle, and Nicholas Coughlin, for showing us how to be better parents.

To Andy Coughlin, for your unwavering love and commitment to feeding us with some of the most amazing food on the planet.

To Scott and Sharron Driscoll, for lending us their lake house for our writing retreats.

To the Earth, which sustains us and makes all things possible.

CHAPTER ONE

Welcoming Complexity into Our Work

"The path isn't a straight line—it is a spiral. You continually come back to things you thought you understood and see deeper truths."

Barry H. Gillespie

Take a moment to consider . . .

What has been your journey in early learning?

What do you think it means to be a pedagogical leader?

What are you hoping for as you begin this book?

We are story sharers, which is slightly different than storytellers.

For years we have been gathering and sharing stories from the early learning classrooms we have had the good fortune to work in and visit. As pedagogical leaders, classroom stories have been one of the most powerful tools we have encountered to help us learn about ourselves, connect with other people, and reflect on practice. So for us it makes sense that we construct our book about pedagogical leadership around stories.

We are also drawn to thinking with structures. Not the kind of rigid structures that do the thinking for you but a variety of open structures that invite questions to help guide, challenge, and expand our thinking.

The stories and structures that we offer in this book are some of the ones we use in our work with the pedagogical leaders and educators in our own organizations and in our consulting work. We offer them to you as an invitation to explore, share, and learn from your own stories of practice.

While we had been toying around with writing together for years, it wasn't until spring 2019 that the ideas for this particular book began to take root. With the encouragement and nudging of our good friend and mentor Deb Curtis, we felt it was time to share some of the thinking and practices that we have found to be so useful over the years. Little could we have known just how much the world was about to change.

Of all the challenges we could have imagined in writing a book, doing it in the middle of a global pandemic wasn't one of them. Like so many others, we have had to learn to move and work differently. It has been a tremendously emotional time during which we have needed to develop new approaches, learn new terminology, rethink budgets, and find creative ways to connect with each other. Yet with all of the loss and challenge that COVID-19 has unleashed on the world, the virus has also offered an opportunity for us to slow down, deeply consider the purpose of our work, and strengthen our resolve to build the kind of world we want to live in. The pandemic has reminded us that we are all global citizens, and our actions have a profound impact on each other and the planet we live on. If there was ever a time for stories of hope and healing in the world, it is now.

In early childhood education, hopefulness has always been our call to action. We have an ethical responsibility to enter our work wearing an armor of optimism. We owe it to children to focus on a future that is worthy of them. To see our challenges as opportunities and leave the world in a better place than we found it. This is our work, and it's why we have written this book.

PEDAGOGY AND PEDAGOGICAL LEADERSHIP

We are living in a rapidly changing world, and as people who live and work with the earth's youngest humans, what we do matters greatly. How might we meet the challenge of our times and work in ways that can help heal the world? How might we reexamine the purpose of education and think more deeply about the kind of educators we want to be? How can we focus our teaching practices around compassion, curiosity, imagination, experimentation, collaboration, innovation, and kindness? We believe the pathway to a new kind of thinking in early childhood is to take a new approach to leadership, one that moves us beyond the administration of rules and regulations and takes a pedagogical approach.

The words *pedagogy* and *pedagogical leader* are relatively new terms for many early childhood educators. Depending on whom you talk to, you will find many different interpretations for each. In education, we think of pedagogy as the study of the teaching and learning processes and the pedagogical leader as someone who supports that study. When we reflect back on our careers, we can see that we were pedagogical leaders long before we knew what the word *pedagogy* meant. As educators in the classroom, we were always curious and eager to understand more about children's learning and thinking.

We intuitively understood that it was our responsibility to create conditions for relationships to unfold. When we moved out of the classroom and into formal leadership roles, we brought that same curiosity and understanding to our work with adults. Over time, we have come to see the role of a pedagogical leader as someone who is curious about thinking and learning, sees the competencies of others, understands the importance of relationships, and develops structures to grow a culture of reflective practice and critical thinking. A pedagogical leader is someone who nurtures learning dispositions and is guided by strong values and a vision for themselves and others.

> *"If I compare a pedagogical leader with a manager, the latter is someone who hovers around and micro-manages to check off a to-do list while the former is a person who shows the direction and vision to follow and also inspires others to research and learn for the sake of personal and professional growth."*
>
> ❧ *Sonya, educator*

We know that for many people, the idea of being a pedagogical leader themselves might be new. Historically, leadership in early childhood has leaned more toward the administrative side. Let's face it, for some folks even pronouncing the word *pedagogy* is a difficult task. Whether your tongue trips over the word or not, if you are interested in growing a culture of reflective thinking in yourself and others, this book is for you. This book is for educators and leaders who are interested in the relationships that unfold through the teaching and learning opportunities that take place every day and how they can become more intentional in their practice. It is for those who want to explore principles that can act as a foundation for their work and who are eager to collaborate and think with others. If this is you, then perhaps you will begin to see yourself as a pedagogical leader as well. While we see that educators in the classroom can take up the role of pedagogical leader alongside children, we have written this book for those leaders who support the work of adults on behalf of their work with young children. We believe all pedagogical leaders deserve a pedagogical leader and an organization that systemically supports this approach.

"My pedagogical leader has definitely shifted my practices as an educator and person. She has helped me build and grow frameworks that challenge my thinking and perspectives."

Carrie, educator

We have experienced firsthand the transformation that takes place when early learning professionals are supported by organizations and leaders who take up a pedagogical approach to their work together. When guided by clear pedagogical principles and intentional practices, educators and pedagogical leaders begin to learn more about themselves and the impact of their work.

THINKING ABOUT QUALITY IN EARLY EDUCATION

It is without question that ensuring quality is one of the greatest responsibilities pedagogical leaders take on. The word *quality* has been part of early childhood rhetoric for as long as we can remember, and for many the pressure to achieve this thing called *quality* is enormous. For years we have been involved in discussions at various tables where dedicated people have searched for the best way to create quality environments. We have been witness to (and, yes, even tried using) a wide variety of checklists, standards, and programs that have been imposed on the early childhood community with the promise of obtaining some kind of "high-quality" experience for children. It seems that every year we are bombarded with some new approach designed to offer a foolproof path to quality. Out of a deep desire to be perceived as a strong and competent educator or leader, we can end up imposing ideas on ourselves and others that have been curated around someone else's perception of quality. All too often these ideas have been narrowly focused around one particular worldview and leave little room for thinking about the role of education and teaching in today's changing world.

With everything leaders are responsible for, it is easy to see how these predesigned approaches can be alluring. And yet, in our combined seventy years of working in this field, we have yet to stumble on any one foolproof standard, checklist, or program that can ensure quality. In fact, we question whether ensuring quality is even possible or ethical. Perhaps it is because there is no one way to think about quality. Quality is complex and personal. It seems to us that asking, "How do we ensure quality?" is not nearly as useful as asking other questions, like "What does quality mean? Who gets to decide? What does quality look, feel, smell, or taste like? Who benefits and who is excluded?" What systems can we design to make sure we include these kinds of questions about quality in all aspects of our organization? Digging into these kinds of questions can help us to see that there are many ideas, many paths, and many stories about quality. The process invites complex thinking and helps us resist the temptation of defining it from a single narrative—one that may benefit only a small portion of the population.

The more we listen to each other, question our certainties, and consider multiple perspectives, the more we come to realize that there is far more about our work (and this world) that we don't know than we do. Being open to each other and different ideas can help us resist leaning toward one universal truth and aid us in realizing that we are continuously learning as we shift and expand our understanding. It can liberate us from thinking that we need to have the one right answer and inspire us to consider other stories. It can shift us from saying "Now we know this" (a declaration of certainty) to "This is what we know now" (an admission that we are continuously shifting and growing and there is no end to our knowing).

When we are willing to embrace the complexity of our work, we become open to many ways of being and we begin to understand that there are many stories and many truths. By suggesting this, we are not implying that anything goes. Instead, we are interested in considering *how* we work together, not simply *what* we produce in our work. We understand that to take up this complex work, we need to develop intentional structures and approaches that invite attention and the time for it.

Over the years, we have come to think more in principles than rules or standards. We believe that principles offer guidance and invite the complexity we need to think about and construct our work. We are interested in contributing to an early learning system that considers more than what is laid out on a developmental checklist or a rating scale. We are interested in a system that considers the kind of classrooms we want to create and the kind of educators and leaders we want to be. We are interested in working toward creating an early learning system where children and adults are seen through a lens of strength. Where we listen to each other and share deep respect for the different ways we can all live in the world. Where issues of equity and social justice are a driving force in our work. We are interested in being a part of an early learning system that considers the impact of its decisions on the land and supports children's inborn connection to the earth. We support a system where educators are intellectually and emotionally engaged alongside children and families. A system of early learning that is eager to grow and learn together, where professional learning is less about training individuals to conform to a prescribed standard of practice and more about growing a profession and programs that are built on becoming better humans. We know that the kind of system we are talking about is grounded in strong values and understands the power of relationships. It is from these beliefs that we identified the four overarching principles that frame the chapters of this book. They act as a guide to help us to consider how we think and learn alongside one another.

- Pedagogical Leaders Work from a Place of Values and Vision
- Pedagogical Leaders Focus on Building Meaningful Relationships
- Pedagogical Leaders See and Support Competence in Children and Adults
- Pedagogical Leaders Support Learning in Multiple Ways by Design

These internalized ideas shape the way we want to make meaning of our work and live our lives. This is not a definitive list of principles. You may well have others. But for us, they encompass the ideas that have emerged from our work. They hold us accountable. They are the touchstones, the foundations that we have come to build our organizational systems and pedagogical practice on. We hope they will do the same for you. While they may seem simple, they are profoundly complex. We like that. These are conceptual ideas that can be pulled apart in many different ways and considered through many perspectives. We don't pretend to be experts on them. We turn to our colleagues to help us. We look to scholars, seek the wisdom of elders, pay attention to artists and philosophers, and most important, learn from the many dedicated educators and pedagogical leaders who have graciously allowed us into their practice. This book is an invitation to join the conversation and explore these ideas with us.

ABOUT THIS BOOK

As pedagogical leaders we are researchers, searching to uncover the practices and approaches that have the greatest positive impact on early childhood practice. We are story sharers, understanding that it is stories that emotionalize our work and engage both our heart and mind. We are system thinkers and inventors, eager to create processes for thinking together. This book reflects each of these parts of us and is constructed around our own research and learning over the past thirty-five years.

We have designed this book so that you can dip into ideas under each principle. There is no need to work through it in a linear way. The principles live within each other and work together. What we have tried to offer is a glimpse into each of them with the hope that you will be inspired to take them up and build on them in a way that makes the most sense to you. Under each of the four principles we have offered some specific ways that pedagogical leaders and educators can bring that principle out in their work. Each section is layered with stories and experiences from our work and highlights many of the practical structures that we have found useful in supporting others. While we have not always used the actual names of programs, educators, and pedagogical leaders we have worked alongside, these stories are a compilation of our collective work together. We hope you see yourself in these stories, and we hope they will inspire each of you, just as they have inspired us.

We offer here some of the many questions and approaches that we have found to be useful for ourselves and for many of the people we work with, but we recognize that everyone's brain understands things a little differently and not everything will work the same for everyone. We encourage you to play around with them and adapt them to your needs. Try them out. Build on them and let them be the catalyst for new questions and structures that can support your own creative and critical thinking. As you come to understand the profound impact of this approach, you will take on the larger and necessary work of advocating for transforming the systems, use of time, budgets, staffing, and professional development to ensure these practices can grow and be sustained.

"As a pedagogical leader, the use of structures has supported my work by providing a way to orient how I move through certain processes. They serve as a compass and bring intention to what I am doing and why. Bringing these structures into my work with others provides clarity and a shared understanding around the work that we are growing together."

Lindsay, pedagogical leader

A LITTLE ABOUT ANNE MARIE

In 1985 I opened the phone book (yes, we used books back then) and called the first child care listed to inquire about a job. When the person on the other end of the phone learned that I was a trained early childhood educator, I was hired sight unseen. No formal interview, no résumé, no onboarding, just a quick tour on my first day to learn where the craft supplies and bathroom were and, *voilà*, I was a preschool teacher. Thirty-five years later, I have dabbled in a few other things. I got married to my life partner, raised three kind, talented children, taught for a while at our local community college, sat on many different boards of directors, and even trained as an herbalist, but I never left that organization.

Thankfully much has evolved over the years, and we don't hire people over the phone anymore. Today London Bridge Child Care Services Inc. is a large multisite nonprofit child care organization located across three counties in southwestern Ontario, Canada. In a way, London Bridge has been a home for me. I feel as though I have grown up there. Over the years I have had the opportunity to work as a center director, professional development coordinator, and director of pedagogy, and today I act as the organization's educational director. One of the reasons I have stayed so long in one place is because that place both has allowed me to grow and has grown along with me.

Of all the possible child care centers I could have called that day, I found the one that would ultimately embrace my consistent need to challenge the status quo. I have a powerful imagination and creative spirit and am constantly conjuring up new projects, alternative approaches, and inventive ways to think about my work. I can imagine how difficult it must have been to work with me when I was younger. I was impatient, and my obsession with finding better ways to do things often stopped me from valuing the hard work and wisdom of the people I spent my days with. Thankfully, through the years I have been blessed with many mentors who have helped me learn to manage my creative unruliness without diminishing my creative spirit. No small task to be sure but one for which I will be forever grateful. My mentors have helped me experience the joy and benefit that comes from collaborating with others and have lovingly nurtured me to discover the values that guide my life. These are the people who have cared enough about me to help me be better. They are the ones who continue to help me learn what it means to be a pedagogical leader. Lorrie McGee Baird is one of those people. Lorrie will have her own story about it, but for me it has been her unwavering persistence that has been the impetus for us to become collaborative partners and cherished friends.

A LITTLE ABOUT LORRIE

I have known since my very early teen years that I wanted to work in early childhood education. After a high school co-op program, I was hooked. I graduated with my ECE diploma in 1985, a time in Ontario when jobs were abundant and in many ways you had a choice of where you wanted to work. I started out at a very small cooperative nursery school, known for its care and innovative practices. The director was Sheila Olan-MacLean, and though I did not know it at that time, she would become an integral part of my career for years to come. Over the next decade I worked in the classroom with various age groups and within different programs, learning from the children, families, and my colleagues along the way. My work at Fleming College lab school launched my work with adults. I was asked to teach a night school class, Early Childhood Methods, to a group of part-time ECE students. I knew then that I wanted to continue to find ways to learn alongside big people on behalf of little people. For the next ten years I continued to grow my career at our local community college and reach out to other communities to provide professional learning opportunities. In 1995, just a few months after the birth of my beautiful baby girl, Kennedy, I received a call from Sheila, who was now working as executive director of a small multisite organization. She was hosting a small conference for her team and invited me to join. She said it was about a new idea she was exploring and thought it was something I would love; the focus was emergent curriculum, and it was being held at a small spa and conference center close by. I must admit, having a new baby at home, the only word I really heard was "spa"! One of the presenters' first slides said, "Teachers should all question their certainties." The conference changed the trajectory of my career, and I never turned back. Fast-forward several years, and Sheila had become the executive director of a larger multisite child care organization, Kawartha Child Care Services, now known as Compass Early Learning and Care. In 2005, I joined the team as a curriculum consultant to support the journey from a theme-based program to a child-centered emergent curriculum. This is where my story with Anne Marie begins.

In the fall of 2005, the Ontario Association for Early Childhood Education held its annual conference in London, Ontario. As part of the conference, participants took tours of a variety of early learning programs. The Stoneybrook site at London Bridge was one of the programs on that tour, and I quickly realized I wanted to learn more about this organization and the person who was leading this work. London Bridge Child Care Services had been exploring practices of emergent curriculum for several years, while our organization was just beginning the journey. It seemed clear from the tour that the two organizations shared a vision and values, both striving to learn more about the conditions and structure that could support an emergent curriculum inspired by the educational philosophy of Reggio Emilia, Italy. After multiple calls and a little persistence on my part, we finally connected. We became fast friends and colleagues in exploring ways to think and learn together. Our relationship continues to grow, and over the years we have become pedagogical leaders for each other, building a network of relationships between our two organizations and inspiring innovative practices that have influenced child care programs across Canada and the United States. Anne Marie is still one of the greatest gifts in both my personal and professional life.

While there are many parts of our lives where we are as different as night and day, when it comes to the values that drive our work, we are steadfastly united. Our experiences as pedagogical leaders of large multisite child care organizations have been remarkably similar, and through our work together over many years we have become valued thinking partners and critical friends. It is for these reasons that this book is written in our shared voice.

OUR OWN LEARNING JOURNEY

Over the years we have been blessed to work alongside and learn from many brilliant and compassionate people who have dedicated their lives to this work. We are grateful for the many opportunities we have been given to experiment with ideas and learn through our own mistakes.

We are humbled by the gifts of patience and understanding we have received from our colleagues as we have stumbled along in our own learning. In particular we are grateful to our own pedagogical leaders who have unwaveringly supported us in our work. While we have had the good fortune to be mentored by many brilliant women, we would be remiss not to acknowledge the influence that Margie Carter and Deb Curtis have had on our work and in our lives.

Many years ago, we were invited to participate as facilitators at an institute that Margie and Deb were doing in Ontario. We had been avid readers of their work and often followed them when they presented at conferences. We were drawn to them because they were some of the first people we had heard who openly spoke about the values that guided their practice. We were inspired by their deep desire to create spaces where educators and children could together be emotionally and intellectually engaged in learning, and we were encouraged by their commitment to reflective practice, collaboration, and perspective sharing. Over time, they also got to know us and invited us to be a part of a network of people they had assembled who held these same values and were committed to the same work. Being a part of this network gave us opportunities to build lasting friendships and collaborate with pedagogical leaders across the United States, becoming fondly known as "the Canadians."

In one of our many retreats together, Margie and Deb invited us to form a line based on when we had become part of this learning community. Each of us one by one formed a line connecting our hands and hearts in this moment of remembering all the experiences we had shared and all that we had learned together. "Look in front of you," they said, "look to those who have offered you mentorship, and look behind you, as these are the people who will look to you." It was a powerful moment. The room stood quiet, with many tears of joy and gratitude shed. We will always remember this moment as a call to action of sorts, a responsibility that every pedagogical leader has for those they mentor. The gifts, the lessons, and the journey each of us takes is to be shared with others so that they too can share with those who follow them. What we know is that every pedagogical leader deserves a pedagogical leader to follow. We will be forever grateful for the mentorship of our dear friends and colleagues Margie Carter and Deb Curtis. We hope you hear their voices in this book, as they have inspired so many of our values and practices.

HOW DO YOU MOVE AN ELEPHANT?

Our work has taken us to many cities, provinces, states, countries, and continents, and we often joke that we have spent more time in planes and hotel rooms together than we have with our own families. We have been graciously invited into schools and child care centers, working alongside educators and emerging pedagogical leaders to bring visibility to the important work that is happening in classrooms around the country.

In our province of Ontario, our organizations have become known for our innovative practices and deep commitment to our pedagogy. In 2012, the Ministry of Education in Ontario had been working toward transforming and modernizing the early learning sector and was beginning to explore a provincial pedagogy to support this work. The ministry had begun a consultation process across the province and invited people to share perspectives on the kinds of things they should be considering. Knowing that we had successfully transformed pedagogical practices across large multisite organizations, they invited us in as part of the consultation process. We were both humbled and honored at the invitation. Rather than explaining any specific thing that we did, we wanted to offer the kinds of questions that we find most helpful in moving thinking and practice.

> What is the nature of the organization and the community we hope to be?
>
> What is the purpose of education?
>
> What is the role of the early childhood educator?
>
> What are our dreams for our classrooms?
>
> How might children contribute to their own learning environments?
>
> How are children portrayed in the environment? What are the stories we tell about them? How are their voices present?
>
> How do children see themselves as part of a community?
>
> How might we think about the role of the organization in professional development as something more than a means to disseminate a prescribed list of strategies and new ideas?
>
> How might we design our organizations to nourish ourselves alongside children and families rather than simply striving to meet requirements?

The most profound thinking in our presentation came from some of the wisest folks we know: children. When we are faced with any momentous task, it can feel like we are trying to move an elephant. Transforming pedagogical practice across a province the size of Ontario is as monumental as you can get, so we asked a group of preschool children for their advice. We asked them, "How do you move an elephant?" Their answers became metaphors for pedagogical leadership.

LILLY SUGGESTED, "You get lots of people to help you pull it."

METAPHOR: You need lots of people with a shared vision in an organization to pull together.

ABDULA SUGGESTED, "You can push his legs."

METAPHOR: To move forward, you need to focus on taking one step at a time.

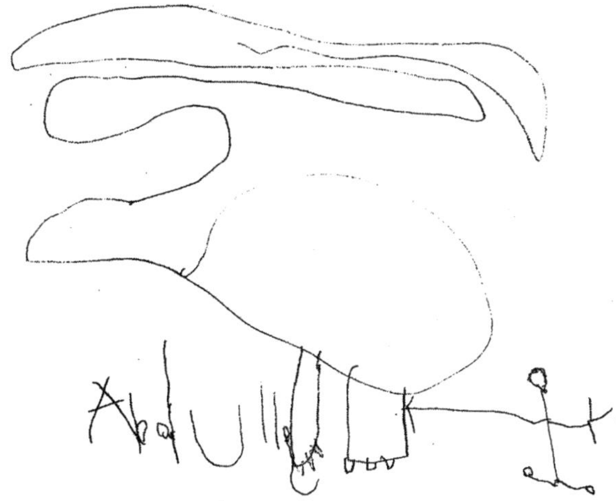

EVAN SUGGESTED, "Find a giant to push the elephant."

METAPHOR: Giants are big and strong, and this is a big job. We need strong people in the lead to help move us along.

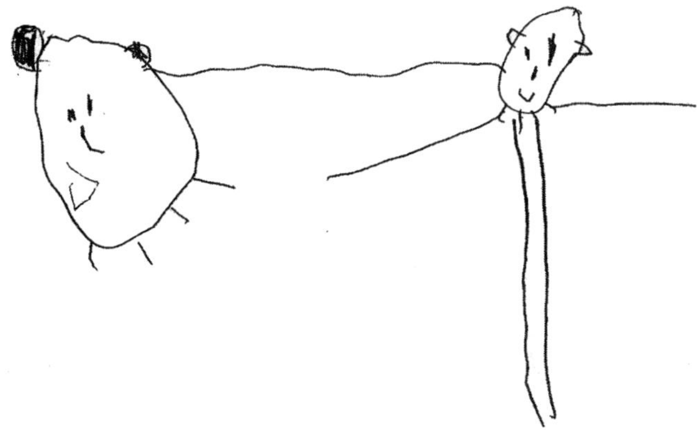

SARAH SUGGESTED, "Elephants like peanuts, so we could leave a trail of peanuts and he might like to follow the way we want him to go."

METAPHOR: Offer incentives built into the organizational systems that people will enjoy along the way.

BEN SUGGESTED, "Scare him."

METAPHOR: Sometimes moving can feel scary.

CHARLIE SUGGESTED, "Ask him nicely."

METAPHOR: Often people just need to be invited to be a part of a change.

HAYDEN SUGGESTED, "He'll move if he wants to. I'll give him toys."

METAPHOR: Ultimately people take action when they see some value in what they are moving to and when they are given the time and resources to move.

Being a pedagogical leader calls us to walk steadfastly toward a future that is brighter for everyone. It asks us to step into something bigger than ourselves. It asks us to resist the ideas that an organization exists to get people to meet the rules and that the leader is the sole knowledge keeper. Instead we are called on to be compassionate listeners, eager learners, innovative inventors, and relentless pursuers of social justice. We hope you will walk alongside us on our journey. Together we can do so much.

CHAPTER TWO

Pedagogical Leaders Work from a Place of Values and Vision

"If you don't know where you're going, it doesn't matter which path you take."

~ *Lewis Carroll,* Alice in Wonderland

Take a moment to consider . . .

What vision do you hold for yourself?

What are the values that underpin your vision?

How do you stay true to these in difficult times?

As pedagogical leaders, we have had the benefit and pleasure of working in our own large multisite organizations as well as countless others across North America. What we have come to understand is, no matter where we visit, regardless of how large or small a child care organization is or how many resources it has access to, early childhood educators have a common desire to create meaningful, supportive spaces for children and families. While we may all define what that looks like differently, our work has shown us that early learning professionals across this continent long to do their best for children, families, and each other.

Understanding their values and having a clear vision of the kind of learning communities they want to build can help pedagogical leaders intentionally nurture the type of early learning environments they dream about. When they invite others to dream with them and articulate a vision for their collective work, it begins to create a road map for taking action. Developing the habit of naming, reflecting on, and deconstructing the beliefs that underpin their vision can help them put into words the values that guide them in their daily practice. When there is both a clear vision and shared values, it becomes a guide for a collective way forward.

Pedagogical leaders . . .

1. Identify values that drive practice.
2. Deconstruct values to better understand them.
3. Align systems and practice with values.
4. Lead with vision.
5. Work to advance equity.

PEDAGOGICAL LEADERS IDENTIFY VALUES THAT DRIVE PRACTICE

Now consider . . .

What are the values that continuously show up in your life?

Where do your values come from?

Having a strong vision can help you clarify the purpose and direction of your work, but it is your values that guide how you live out your daily practice. It is not uncommon for early learning programs to create value statements. Often they can be found strategically posted at an entrance or declared on a website. However, having a set of values and living by them are two different things. It is relatively easy to create a value statement, but to design a space where specific values are visible takes awareness, intentionality, and an understanding of the complexity of the endeavor.

Whether we have identified them by name or not, we all have underlying beliefs that influence how we live our lives. Our past experiences, culture, and upbringing can have a powerful influence on the kinds of things we come to believe are important. These underlying beliefs shape our values and influence how we engage and communicate with each other. They can affect everything from the clothes we wear to how we spend our time and money to the kinds of things we give our attention to.

"Naming my values has shifted my practice. It has given clarity and accountability to my thoughts and everyday actions. As a leader, having clarity of my values not only keeps me grounded but passionate about my work and what I believe and stand for. Staying true to my values and beliefs, I bring my best self to work and I know that I am on the path I was meant to be on."

Lisa, pedagogical leader

When pedagogical leaders can recognize and name the values that drive their own practice, they are better able to understand why they do what they do. They in turn can assist educators who might have difficulty in identifying the values that motivate them. While it is important to have a set of shared values to work from, different values can guide each of us at different times. The role of the pedagogical leader is not to ensure that everyone gets on the same page or works from the exact same values all the time. A diverse learning community will always bring with it a variety of ways of being and thinking. Instead, a pedagogical leader can talk about the values that drive educators in different circumstances and consider how those values align with the larger vision of the organization. A pedagogical leader can also help ensure that values stay relevant as an organization evolves. For example, as awareness grows around important issues that face communities today, such as systemic racism and climate change, it can start to awaken a deeper sense of caring in people and bring new values to the forefront. In an effort to support educators in understanding how their environment reflects their values, pedagogical leaders can take up the practice of noticing where values live in their spaces. In our organizations we understand that carving out time to think together is critical, so we encourage pedagogical leaders to think differently about how to use it. Rather than using staff meetings as a way to disseminate administrative updates, pedagogical leader Diane took advantage of this time to think together with the team about the values that were conveyed in their environments. Observe how Diane used a staff meeting to invite a discussion around values.

Diane invited all of the educators from her program to stand in the entrance of their center and then used a series of questions to get the group to reflect on what they saw. She asked:

What do you see?

What messages does our entranceway give to families, educators, and community?

What does it show that we value?

How does it align or misalign with what we want for children, families, and ourselves?

At first look the group noticed that there was a vision statement beautifully written on the wall of the entranceway. There was a chair for families to sit on, books and materials to read, and a table of pamphlets and information to take away. Initially, the educators felt that the space conveyed to families the feelings of being welcomed, informed, and engaged, a place to linger and relax. These were all values they wanted for families. However, as they moved into the main lobby of their building, they began to see there were other messages they didn't necessarily feel comfortable about. They noticed the many posters on the walls competing for attention. As they walked through the space they felt bombarded with information about the importance of immunization, seat belt safety, and using sunscreen and why you should never leave your child unattended in a car. A formal reception desk took up a large part of the space, and at least four different signs indicated how and when parents could pay their child care bill.

Looking together at this space with a critical eye helped educators notice that the dominant values conveyed here were misaligned with what they wanted. While these other messages were well intentioned, what they really wanted for families to feel right away is that they belonged. They wanted it to be clear to anyone setting foot into the building that this was a place where children are held in high regard, where educators are constantly learning and know that parents are important partners. The conversation sparked a great deal of reflection, and the team started to think of creative ideas to welcome families in a more thoughtful way. They created a much smaller area for public health information and put up images of families and children interacting together with educators. They replaced the single chair with two smaller, more comfortable ones to invite conversation, and they replaced the large reception desk with a smaller table and some large plants.

Moving through this process together helped the educators consider some of the subtle ways that values reveal themselves. Diane then invited educator teams to do the same thing in their own classrooms. Educators took multiple photos of their spaces and brought them to team meetings. Together with Diane, they studied their classroom images and asked themselves the same questions they used to consider the values in the center entrance.

Studying photos of environments is a useful way to revisit the intentional and unintentional values that might be conveyed in your space. It can also help both pedagogical leaders and educators

- notice what they are drawn to,
- consciously name the values that stand out for them,
- bring visibility to what they believe and value,
- understand others' points of view,
- consider the value that is present in their initial response, and
- consider the value they would want to drive their response.

Pause and Reflect

How does your space at home or at work reflect your values?

What messages does it convey to others?

Exploring Your Own Practice: Naming Values

Your values are present in everything you do—from the way you set up your environments to how you engage with each other, families, and children. The following structure can be useful in helping pedagogical leaders and educators uncover their own shared values and consider some questions that can help align those values to their practice.

Reflect on the following list of values and feel free to add other ideas that you feel belong. Invite educators to consider the list together, and choose six values that are most important to them in their classroom.

Accountability
Accuracy
Achievement
Altruism
Ambition
Assertiveness
Balance
Belonging
Boldness
Calmness
Carefulness
Challenge
Cheerfulness
Commitment
Community
Compassion
Consistency
Contentment
Contribution
Control
Cooperation
Courtesy
Creativity
Curiosity
Decisiveness
Dependability
Determination
Devoutness
Diligence
Discipline
Discretion
Diversity
Effectiveness
Efficiency
Empathy
Enthusiasm
Equity
Excellence
Excitement
Expertise
Exploration
Expressiveness
Fairness
Faith
Family
Fidelity
Fitness
Fluency
Focus
Freedom
Fun
Generosity
Grace
Growth
Happiness
Hard Work
Harmony
Health
Helpfulness
Holiness
Honesty
Honor
Humility
Independence
Ingenuity
Insightfulness
Intelligence
Joy
Justice
Leadership
Legacy
Love
Loyalty
Mastery
Openness
Order
Originality
Perfection
Positivity
Practicality
Preparedness
Professionalism
Prudence
Reflection
Reliability
Resourcefulness
Restraint
Rigor
Security
Self-control
Selflessness
Self-reliance
Sensitivity
Serenity
Simplicity
Spontaneity
Stability
Strategic Thinking
Strength
Structure
Success
Teamwork
Temperance
Thankfulness
Thoroughness
Thoughtfulness
Timeliness
Tolerance
Trustworthiness
Understanding
Uniqueness
Unity
Vitality

www.redleafpress.org/crp/d-1.pdf

Invite educators to consider how these values are

- visible in the way they design their environment for children;
- present in daily routines and rituals;
- considered in their relationships with each other, children, families, the community, and the Earth; and
- connected to the vision of the classroom, program, or organization.

As a pedagogical leader, consider how your values are

- visible in how you set up spaces for educators;
- present in how you structure meetings and time to work side by side with educators;
- considered in the relationships you have with others, the community, and the Earth;
- connected to the vision of the classroom, program, or organization; and
- shared throughout the organization.

Whether you are an educator choosing your response to children or a pedagogical leader choosing your response to educators, having clarity about your values can help you resist using power and position to make decisions. Instead of relying on gut reactions, your responses are guided by the kind of community you want to build and the values that drive your practice. Naming the values that guide your practice is not always an easy task. It requires a willingness for self-reflection, an openness to hearing different points of view, a desire to understand what values look like in practice, and a willingness to make changes in the bureaucracy.

PEDAGOGICAL LEADERS DECONSTRUCT VALUES TO BETTER UNDERSTAND THEM

Now consider . . .

How often do you think about your values in your daily practice?

What do you notice about the shared values you and others hold?

Have you ever been surprised at how two people can think differently about the same value?

Naming your values is the first step in understanding what you and those around you believe is important. However, declaring a belief in something is often easier than living it. It is not as simple as declaring a list of values, putting them on the wall, and then expecting everyone to follow along in a particular way. A pedagogical leader can help make the link between values and practice for both themselves and the educators they work with. This is daily work that requires constant attention and consideration. There is never one right way to live a value. Different people often think differently about the same value. It is not the role of the pedagogical leader to determine the right interpretation but instead to notice the differences and invite dialogue and reflection.

Consider the idea of strong relationships as a shared value. In order for strong relationships to exist, there needs to be a common understanding of what having a strong relationship with someone, or something, means. It calls us to consider questions like the following:

What is required of us to have a strong relationship with someone?

Who gets to decide what a strong relationship looks like?

Can I have a strong relationship with someone I don't particularly like?

How can relationships thrive during times of conflict?

With whom or what do we want to build strong relationships?

How do we nurture a strong relationship with the Earth and other living things?

Clearly it is not as simple as declaring that strong relationships are an important value. Uncovering what that means in different situations requires reflection, understanding, and self-awareness.

When pedagogical leaders use questions like these to engage educators in conversations, they can help uncover the different perspectives and interpretations that naturally exist among people. They help create a space where thoughtful dialogue can happen and a greater clarity and understanding about the shared values that guide their practice begins to take root. Once this happens, it is much easier to see where practice either aligns or misaligns with these shared beliefs. For example, risk-taking is a value that has many different interpretations. How risk-taking is defined and understood can have a huge impact on how that value influences a person's practice. Inviting individuals to consider questions like "How do I define risk-taking?" or "What from my experiences is influencing my feelings about risk-taking?"

can help individuals articulate their own understanding and reasoning. Once this happens it becomes easier to see similarities and differences between how people think about the same value. Taking time to have conversations with educators about values and what they mean to different people can help them understand why their response is sometimes different than their coworkers'.

Consider how a group of preschool educators found themselves in conflict around the rules and expectations they had for the children on their playground. Several of the educators allowed the children to walk along a three-foot-tall brick wall that surrounded the gardens in the playground. They saw the children's excitement and eagerness to challenge their bodies and believed that children deserved to have these kinds of experiences.

Others considered this too dangerous and would continuously ask the children to get down off the wall. Over time this fundamental difference in expectations caused problems for both children and educators. Educators imposed their own rules on the children in their group even though they were all sharing the playground at the same time. Some children were allowed to climb on the wall while others were not, causing ill feelings among the children and judgment and resentment among the educators.

Pause and Reflect

Have you ever interpreted a value differently than a coworker?

What do you do when this happens?

As tensions over this risk-taking on the playground mounted, the center's pedagogical leader Elaine planned a meeting with the preschool educators to talk about what was happening. She began by naming what she saw.

> I notice that there are different ideas about the children climbing on the garden wall.
>
> There seems to be some tension and confusion around it.
>
> There seem to be some competing values at play here around risk-taking and safety.

By naming her observations, Elaine set up a space to talk about them. The educators began to share their perspectives about safety and defend their decisions. Emotions were high, as each of them believed they had the best interest of the children in mind. At this point Elaine offered some questions to help the educators consider what they actually wanted for the children:

What does it mean to keep children safe?

Is it possible to keep children too safe?

What is the value of risk-taking?

What is the difference between something that is risky and something that is dangerous?

How does your own fear affect the experience of the children?

What are the children showing you about their competencies here?

What other considerations should be made besides safety and risk-taking?

These questions changed the dynamics of the conversation. They helped the educators move beyond their initial emotional responses to the situation and think more about the implications of their decisions. The kinds of questions that Elaine offered helped the educators move from defending their practice to exploring it. Their conversations helped them identify their own fears about children getting hurt while in their care and prompted some to admit that saying no is the easiest way to ensure safety. The educators who supported the children's desire to climb on the wall were able to acknowledge that without appropriate guidance and supervision, the activity could be dangerous for children.

As their conversations unfolded and they listened to each other, it became clear that they all actually saw value in children's risk-taking and they all wanted the children to be safe. Acknowledging this in each other helped the educators to shift away from the simple question of whether the children should or should not be allowed to climb on the wall and instead ask:

What conditions need to be met to enable children to climb on the wall?

How do we supervise the children's climbing and who is best to do it?

The conversations about the risks on the playground were so insightful for the educators that they prompted a center-wide investigation to consider what other kinds of risk-taking children engage in naturally besides physical risks. In the end, this initial conflict of values turned into a collective multi-year center-wide study on how to grow risk competence in young children.

It can be easy in situations like this to impose a rule that everyone must follow. However, a pedagogical leader can use these kinds of conflicts to help educators name their values, notice practice, and consider the implications of their decisions.

Exploring Your Own Practice: Considering Conflicting Values

When people's values seem to conflict, this tension can stifle partnerships and cause stress and confusion. Conflict can also offer an opportunity to think more reflectively about people's beliefs, uncover shared understandings, and consider what values look like in practice.

The next time you notice tensions caused by conflicting values, try using the following questions to invite reflection and dialogue and plan a way forward.

www.redleafpress.org/crp/d-2.pdf

Considering Conflicting Values	
Notice & Name Bring attention to the situation by naming out loud what you notice.	• What different beliefs or values do you think might be at play here? • What specific things do you see happening? • What are you noticing about how people are talking with or responding to each other? • What kinds of decisions are being made? • How might the organization's requirements and resources be contributing to the conflict? • How do you think people are feeling?
Share & Interpret Share what is noticed with others and interpret together possible implications or consequences.	• Why is this value important? • What other values might be considered here? • How are our interpretations of this value similar? Different? • Are there other ways to interpret this value? • What is the impact of my actions or decisions on children, coworkers, families, and the Earth when I act from this value? • What is the impact of the organizational systems on how the value is being interpreted?
Identify Action How will you respond to what you are learning together?	• What new questions might you ask as a result of this conversation? • What new conversations do you want or need to have? • What specific action might you want to take here?

A conflict of values can happen between two or more people or even within one person. The organization and program policies and approaches may also create these conflicts in values. An educator may see value in children taking risks, but safety may loom larger in that moment and so they respond by stopping a child's experience. In any given situation, there are always multiple ways in which an educator might respond to a child or a pedagogical leader might respond to an educator. Competing values can cause conflict, or they can create a space for growth. Rather than prescribing a singular right way, pedagogical leaders understand that the best response is a thoughtful one that considers both the present moment and a bigger vision. Regularly reflecting on the values that guide practice and the organization can help both educators and pedagogical leaders work with purpose and intention rather than simply repeating scripts and routines.

Consider how Kelly, a pedagogical leader from a multisite child care organization, helped school-age educator Luis deconstruct the values that influenced how he set up materials for children.

During a scheduled visit, Kelly paused to observe Luis in his after-school program. In the center of the room she noticed a large round table that Luis had carefully prepared with materials to invite children into play. Pencils and clipboards with white paper were placed at every seat, and measuring and weighing tools were thoughtfully arranged in the center of the table. A small group of children had joined together and were engaged in lively conversation, exploring the materials and writing and drawing their ideas. The experience lasted for some time until a new idea seemed to spark their interest, and they quickly left the table and joined another group of children across the room.

Luis had been watching the group, and as soon as he noticed their departure, he quickly went over to the table and restaged the experience. He sorted the materials, added new paper to the clipboards, inspected the pencils to see if they needed to be sharpened, and pushed in the chairs. The invitation for play was now ready for a new group of children.

At the end of the day Kelly connected with Luis and asked him about the role he played in restaging the materials and was curious about what his thinking was behind this practice. His response was simply, "Oh, that's just what I do."

Pause and Reflect

Are there things that you do without really thinking about them?

Is this a common response that you notice? Why do you think this is?

Wanting him to reflect a little more, Kelly urged Luis to talk about why he made the decision to restage the table. After a short pause, he stated, "I believe that every child deserves to have beautiful materials that are arranged to invite them into play. I see it as my role to restage these invitations so that children can continue in their play as new ideas come to them. We come together at the end of the day to tidy our space, but asking children to tidy up after every experience often interrupts their thinking. I guess I have never really thought about it. It's just what I do."

Several weeks later, when Luis and Kelly met up again he said, "You know that thing we talked about . . . the restaging of materials? I find myself doing it all the time now, and I am really noticing the children seem to be more engaged and the environment feels more settled." What had become clear to Kelly was that by encouraging Luis to consider the values that guided why he did what he did, it moved his practice from habit to intention. When pedagogical leaders take time with educators to pause and leave breathing room to reflect, the values that guide them in their work can become clearer over time.

Each day we make decisions about how we are going to live and learn alongside children. Although restaging in this way may not be your practice, the idea is to continually take time to reflect on why we do what we do and the values we are trying to grow in our work. Identifying the values that guide you is the first step. Our life's work then becomes learning how those values translate to practice. Once you have identified the values that guide you, you can move away from habitual or reactive responses and grow more intentional in your practice. Pedagogical leaders can help educators see how their practice aligns with the values they want to encourage in their classrooms.

> *"Giving voice to my values and stopping to consider how I want to be with children and how I show up for children is vital. Self-reflection isn't a one-and-done checklist; it is an ever-evolving knowledge of self. It is being acutely aware of the guideposts of your daily experience."*
>
> ~ *Kirsty, pedagogical leader*

Exploring Your Own Practice: Deconstructing Values

While individuals will undoubtedly hold a variety of values, there are some values that should be nonnegotiable in early childhood settings. Among them are values that support antibias education such as diversity, inclusion, and equity. While these words are finding their way more and more in our early childhood vocabulary, it is important that we understand what they mean. Each of these values work together but are not synonymous. As we think with them, we continue to learn more about what they ask of us.

Diversity focuses on representation and who is present. It is relational and shows up in groups. People alone aren't diverse; the communities they belong to are.

Inclusion addresses the quality of the experience that people in a group have. It is the degree to which someone can fully benefit from and participate in what the group is offering. For example, a classroom that has people with many different identities may be diverse, but that does not make it inclusive. Inclusivity happens when each of those people is able to fully participate and take advantage of the benefits that the classroom has to offer.

Equity acknowledges that different people have had different experiences and have different needs. Equity seeks to even the playing field and disrupts the idea that *fairness* means *equal*.

How do these definitions of diversity, inclusion, and equity connect with how you think about them?

What do you think about each of these ideas in your daily practice?

What are you doing to learn more about advancing diversity, inclusion, and equity in your practice?

Here are a few other values that we find many educators and pedagogical leaders agree on.

- Curiosity
- Well-being
- Risk-Taking
- Trust

Consider these values (or others that are important to you). Use the following questions to think about each of them with educators:

How do I define this value?

What about my experiences is influencing how I consider this value?

How does it show up for me in my daily practice?

How does my program support or discourage this value?

When is it hard for me to practice this value?

Now consider together:

What are the similarities and differences in the way we think about each of these values?

What are the common practices that we have connected to each of these values?

What new ways have we come to think about each of these values as a result of our conversations?

How might our administrative policies and procedures support us to live our values together?

As pedagogical leaders work together with educators to understand the values that influence and drive their practice, educators work with children to understand the values that they want to influence their classroom culture.

Consider these values again, only this time think about specific ways that pedagogical leaders and educators might nurture them in themselves, in children, and in each other.

Value: Curiosity	• In what ways can educators nurture children's natural curiosity about the world around them? • In what ways can pedagogical leaders nurture educators' curiosity about children's learning? • In what ways can pedagogical leaders and educators nurture their own curiosity? • What role can the organization play in nurturing curiosity about everyone's learning?
Value: Well-being	• In what ways can educators invest in the well-being of children and support their growing sense of self? • In what ways do pedagogical leaders invest wholeheartedly in the well-being of educators? • In what ways can pedagogical leaders and educators invest in their own wellness? • What role can the organization invest in to ensure well-being of all its members?
Value: Risk-Taking	• How do educators grow resilience and opportunities to try things out and take risks with children? • How do pedagogical leaders provide opportunities for educators to take risks and try out new ideas? • In what ways can pedagogical leaders and educators nurture their own disposition to take risks? • What role can the organization play to nurture dispositions for risk-taking?
Value: Trust	• How do educators build trust with children? • How do pedagogical leaders build trust with educators? • How do pedagogical leaders and educators come to trust themselves? • How does the organization build trust with all its members?

www.redleafpress.org/crp/d-3.pdf

Identifying the shared values that guide practice doesn't mean that everyone will start to agree and live in harmony together. Instead, the act of naming values is only the beginning. Declaring values offers pedagogical leaders and educators an opportunity to reflect, listen, and ultimately adopt practices that align with what they are trying to grow.

PEDAGOGICAL LEADERS ALIGN PRACTICE WITH VALUES

Now consider . . .

How do you know when your values are aligned with your practice?

What happens when they are misaligned?

When pedagogical leaders align their values to their practice, they become a living example of these values. Aligning your actions with your values takes intention. It is easy to make thoughtful decisions when things are running smoothly, but it can be much more difficult when situations are heightened or when you feel competing pressures. Pedagogical leaders are human—and part of being human means you don't always get it right. Having clarity about the values that drive your practice helps enable you to notice when your actions are misaligned with what you believe. Even when there is clarity about values, misalignments can happen. And when this happens, pedagogical leaders can use the misalignment as a valuable opportunity for learning and building relationships. Consider what happened when this pedagogical leader responded to a misalignment in her values and actions.

Karla, a new pedagogical leader, had been thinking with Ben and Ida about how they might rearrange their preschool classroom to be more inviting for the children. All three of them had noticed that things were feeling a little stagnant for both the educators and the children and wanted to start to consider some different ways they could think about the classroom space.

Recognizing that Ben and Ida were very busy with different things going on in the classroom, Karla decided that she would come into the center in the evening and rearrange the classroom for them. As a pedagogical leader, she had a clear idea in her mind about how she could arrange the space in a way that would engage the children and be interesting for the adults. The next morning when Ben and Ida came into the classroom, Karla had expected to see gratitude and excitement for all she had done. Instead, the educators seemed silent and dismayed. Karla had hoped they would be spending the morning talking about all the exciting changes, but the educators were angry and not interested in talking with her at all.

Pause and Reflect

Do you ever find that your well-intentioned responses are not welcomed? How do you react when this happens?

At first, Karla found herself getting defensive, but she caught herself and paused. She approached Ben and Ida and said, "Clearly I have done something that has upset you. I am wondering if you would be willing to talk with me about it at our team meeting." Ben and Ida agreed, and at their team meeting Karla began by acknowledging that she had upset them. She then asked if the educators would share what had bothered them, and she listened. While Karla had not intended to exclude or make the educators feel like their ideas were not important, she had realized that her actions in this situation did not align with her values. Karla valued collaboration. She believed in working side by side with educators and wanted them to take a lead and be active participants in classroom decisions. She realized that by going into the classroom without them, she had robbed Ida and Ben of the experience of participating in the process and adding their perspectives.

As she continued to listen, Karla learned more about Ben's and Ida's points of view. She sat quietly and then acknowledged the impact her decision had on the team. She apologized and asked how she might have approached the situation differently. At the end of their conversation, she thanked Ben and Ida for being open with her and repeated what she heard them say. Then she asked the educators if they could start again, this time working together. Ben and Ida agreed.

Pause and Reflect

In what ways do you think Karla's actions misaligned with her values?

What specific things did you notice her doing and saying to respond to her own misalignment?

How might the organizational systems support Karla's practice as a pedagogical leader in a situation like this one?

Pedagogical leaders understand that their character is revealed through their daily encounters. Educators learn quickly what they can expect from their leaders by watching how they respond or react in different situations. Strong relationships are built when educators can trust that their leaders will respond from their values regardless of the situation.

Admittedly, aligning actions with values is not always easy or convenient. Especially when situations become difficult, it can seem easier to use power and position to enforce something rather than to take the time to listen to different perspectives, negotiate, collaborate, or compromise. For example, when conflict arises between two working partners who seem to have vastly different ideas, the pedagogical leader has a choice. They can impose a solution or assist their coworkers in working through the problem. Both of these responses provide educators with insight into what they can expect from their pedagogical leader:

Conflicts are an important part of being in a relationship together. We listen to each other and work through conflicts.

or

When conflicts become too difficult, I will take the responsibility and make the decision.

Pedagogical leaders demonstrate what is important to them by how they approach these kinds of situations. While facilitating conflicts can be challenging and take time, the pedagogical leader who values relationships understands that they are built by working through the difficult times as well as through the pleasant ones. They recognize that trust or mistrust grows through daily encounters. Educators learn to either share their thinking openly or simply say what their leader wants to hear. They learn to second-guess and doubt or believe that their pedagogical leader is invested in their success and well-being. They come to learn this not so much through what their pedagogical leader says but by watching how they live. Trust flourishes when educators witness their pedagogical leaders embrace and take responsibility for their slipups. They come to trust that it is OK to make mistakes and that they are a critical part of learning. It could have been easy for Karla to use her power and position to defend her decision to set up the room without Ben and Ida. Instead, she allowed her values of collaboration and teacher initiative to guide her response. She openly acknowledged the impact of her mistake and asked if they could try again.

Consciously aligning actions to values can take practice. It can be easy to move throughout the day on autopilot, not always thinking about the impact of your response on others. As a pedagogical leader, your beliefs and expectations are communicated moment by moment by what you do far more than by what you say.

"Naming my values has allowed me the opportunity to slow down and reflect on what and—more important—why my values are what they are. Although I find it to be a complex and messy process to name my values, going through the process has guided me to move through my practice with more intention. My values have become a warm, comfortable place that I trust when the profession presents difficult challenges; I often look to those values when I need to regroup. It is a process that I always work through when beginning work with a new team of educators."

Julie, pedagogical leader

Exploring Your Own Practice: Connecting Values and Practice

Consciously set aside a day or part of a day to intentionally pay attention to how you respond to different situations. See if you can name the value attached to your responses. Write about what you are noticing.

What types of situations are easy for you to connect a value to?

What situations are more difficult?

Do you notice any misalignments between your responses and your values?

Use the following structure to help you notice connections and disconnections between your actions and your values.

www.redleafpress.org/crp/d-4.pdf

A value that I hold	What I notice about how my practice aligns with this value	What I notice about how my practice misaligns with this value

PEDAGOGICAL LEADERS USE VALUES TO GROUND THEIR VISION

Now consider . . .

What is the purpose of your work?

What do you envision for the learning environment you want to create?

While your eyes may give you vision to see what is in front of you, it is your imagination that enables you to see what is not yet there. Leading with vision means having unwavering clarity about the kind of learning environment you aspire to create and the kind of people you wish to be. Having clarity helps you imagine for yourself the role you play in supporting your own practice and the practice of the educators you work with. Just as you lead from a vision, you encourage others to do the same in their own work. A strong vision is often born from our values and a strong desire for something different than you currently have. As a pedagogical leader, it can help both you and the educators you work with to create a more intentional, reflective, and thoughtful approach together.

It is without question that visioning new possibilities for yourself is a worthy way to use your time and energy, but admittedly it is not always easy. It requires pedagogical leaders to take notice of and sometimes disrupt habitual ways of thinking. It challenges educators to see beyond what they have to what could be. It demands a sense of hopefulness and optimism. This process takes practice and discipline and thinking with others. Let's face it, pedagogical leaders and educators are busy people. Even when they do manage to squeak out a little time to exercise their imagination and consider something different, it can be easy to fall victim to one or more of the many barriers that stop them from creating a new vision. Barriers can feel very real for both pedagogical leaders and educators and can sometimes make dreaming feel like it is a waste of time.

> I barely have enough time to get my work done in a day. I don't have time to dream.
>
> I don't have the resources I need now.
>
> It's difficult to find time to meet with educators and other pedagogical leaders to talk about our work.
>
> I feel pulled in a thousand directions.

While these and many other barriers may feel very real, it may be helpful to remember that dreaming is different than doing. It requires no special funding, no added resources, and no special skills, save an alert and active imagination. The first steps toward meaningful change always begin in the mind.

In its simplest form, visioning is the act of imagining something better for ourselves, and we would argue that it is critical for any effective leader working with adults and children. Exercising your imagination can ignite the dreamer in you and help you be more effective as a pedagogical leader. It can also help reveal areas where you can get stuck, enabling you to become more aware of your own barriers and see the possibilities that lay beyond them. It does the same thing for educators.

Watch how using questions helped us move through some common barriers around visioning. We recall a time where we asked a group of educators to imagine what they wanted for themselves and their classrooms. They shared that they dreamed of a work environment where their coworkers weren't late for their shifts, where children didn't have behavior problems, and where parents wouldn't forget to bring in diapers for their children. In other words, their biggest dreams hinged on the notion that other people needed to change. As we dug further into the question, we noticed that the group seemed to dwell on problems rather than imagining possibilities. When we noticed these things together, we learned that there was a hesitation to dream big because big dreams can feel impossible. Their thought clearly was, "Best not to waste time dreaming about something that could never happen."

Pause and Reflect

Do you spend much time dreaming about possibilities in your work?

What kind of things do you dream about?

Does the reality of what you currently have ever get in the way of your dreams?

When we reflected together on the barriers that had come up for this group of educators, we were able to identify that they seemed to revolve around feelings of lack. Lack of time, lack of resources and money, and, yes, lack of imagination. Some even indicated that dreaming was scary because it just reminded them of what they didn't have. In a world that is so focused on productivity, dreaming can seem like a time waster.

We recognized that simply asking the question "What do you imagine for yourself?" wasn't enough to generate new thinking. We needed to offer a way to imagine something different. We invited them to go back and try again, but this time we offered a way to think through it. We asked them to consider:

> How do you want to feel when you come to work?
>
> What do you want children, families, and coworkers to feel?
>
> What do you want to learn more about, and what strengths can you draw on?
>
> What kind of community do you want to help build?

The educators' answers to these questions helped inform the purpose of their work, giving it importance and meaning. The kinds of questions pedagogical leaders ask matter. Questions can open up minds and ignite new thinking, or they can confuse and cause defensiveness and feelings of judgment. Sometimes broad questions can feel overwhelming and out of reach. When pedagogical leaders ask educators more specific questions, it can help them carve out a clearer vision. When educators have stronger clarity around the kinds of things they envision for themselves, children, families, and their communities, it helps them make more intentional decisions around what they do.

The following structure can help both pedagogical leaders and educators work through a process to clarify a particular vision, create a plan, reflect on what they are learning, and evolve rather than simply repeat the same practices. This structure can be useful in planning specific projects, events, and experiences or in considering an overall direction.

Exploring Your Own Practice: Visioning Together

Dream, Do, Reflect, Evolve, Repeat	
Dream	• What specific dream, goal, or vision do you have for yourself or your classroom, program, or organization? • What values ground your work here? • Why is this dream important for you and for others? • What impact do you hope this has? • What other possibilities exist for learning or relationship building?
Do	• What are some specific things you might put in place that will help you move toward your dream? • What mindsets, skills, or knowledge might be required to do this? • What are the unique strengths that different educators can bring? • What tools or resources will you need? • What professional development might be required? • What individual responsibilities will people take? • What are your timelines? • How will you stay on track?
Reflect	• What specifically do you see happening as a result of your efforts? • Did you get the results you were hoping for? • What didn't happen that you thought would? • What is your theory about that? • What have you learned about yourself and others? • What do you want to remember for next time?
Evolve	• What new ideas and questions were generated? • How can you share with others what you have discovered? • What new dreams have been born from this process?
Repeat	• Work through the process again, adding any new considerations or insights that you have discovered.

www.redleafpress.org/crp/d-5.pdf

Watch how a pedagogical leader used this structure for visioning to support educators who were struggling in their lively preschool classroom.

Debbie and Gina's classroom had been set up so that some children came for the morning, some came for the afternoon, and others attended the full day. This schedule had meant that all the children were together over lunch. Instead of being a nourishing gathering time, lunchtime in this preschool room was a wild frenzy of continuous head counting, rushing children to eat, checking and double-checking belongings, getting little ones on and off the right buses, scraping dishes, cleaning faces, and futile attempts to get children on their cots for nap. It was an exhausting and stressful time for all involved.

At one of their team meetings, pedagogical leader Marie asked Debbie and Gina, "What do you wish lunchtime could be like?" They responded by sharing everything they tried and how it didn't work. They seemed resigned to the fact that this was their reality and there was no changing it. With a little nudging, and some different questions, Marie was able to encourage them to dream a little. She asked them, "What do you love about sharing a meal with others? What is important to you about sharing a meal together? How are relationships and a sense of community built when we share a meal together?"

Pause and Reflect

Is there any part of your day you wish could change?

What questions might you ask yourself that could help you start to envision something different?

It would have been easy for Marie as a pedagogical leader to tell educators what they could do to relieve some of the chaos in their classroom. She could have advocated for more resources or even initiated new policies or rules about when and how children came into the space. However, by asking different questions, she resisted telling the educators what they should do and invited them instead to consider what they wanted and why they wanted it. This approach helps nurture critical and reflective thinking and can empower educators to take action and effect change.

By the end of their conversation, they were able to articulate specific ideas about why gathering together around food is important. They were able to identify what they longed for and the potential that existed for everyone around this important time of day. They turned those ideas into a declaration and wrote it out neatly on a crisp piece of card stock and stuck it on the wall in the dining room.

It read,

> Mealtime is a sacred time for us to come together as a classroom community. It is a time to nourish our bodies as well as our hearts and minds. It is a time for building relationships and to feel a sense of belonging.

The next day, it was chaos as usual, with one difference. Although no one was quite sure how they would do it, there was a clear vision of what they hoped for. Having this newfound clarity slowly started to have an impact. While children were still coming and going, Debbie and Gina found themselves talking differently. Instead of rushing children and throwing out a barrage of questions about where they should be and what they should be doing, they took inspiration from their own declaration and started to have conversations with children.

As their pedagogical leader, Marie started to name the shifts she saw happening in both the educators and the children. She noticed that Debbie and Gina were both sitting at the table, sharing a meal with the children rather than busily serving and scraping plates. She noticed how eager the children were to have conversations with each other and brought attention to the shifting energy in the room. Slowly stress levels started to lessen as children and educators began to work together in setting up and cleaning up the meal.

By bringing attention to these small shifts, Marie helped educators notice the impact of their own attitudes and actions. This inspired them to make intentional changes to their practice that in turn helped change the mealtime experience for everyone.

Over a few short weeks, lunchtime became one of the most enjoyable times of day for everyone. The experience was such a powerful one for the educators that it inspired them to repeat this process in other areas and aspects of their classroom.

Revisit how the structure for visioning helped to transform the lunchtime experience in Debbie and Gina's classroom.

Dream, Do, Reflect, Evolve, Repeat	
Dream	• The pedagogical leader asked specific questions to help the educators form a picture in their mind and articulate their vision for a meaningful shared lunch experience. • Declaring a vision for lunchtime reinforced its value and importance. It provided educators with clarity about what they wanted to pay attention to.
Do	• They started by writing down what they wanted lunchtime to look like and why. • Educators sat and engaged with children at the lunch table. • They used conversational instead of directional language with the children. • They began to include children in lunchtime tasks.
Reflect	• The pedagogical leader noticed and named the small shifts in educators' attitudes and the specific things they did differently. Together they reflected on how their decisions and behavior affected the children and the stress level of the classroom.
Evolve	• New mealtime practices were defined and implemented.
Repeat	• The educators understood how the process worked and were able to repeat it in different areas of the classroom.

The stories shared here illustrate how a pedagogical leader can work together with educators to help articulate the purpose of their work and invite them into the kind of dialogue and reflection that moves practice. Practice using the structure for visioning at your next staff or team meeting. What happens when you take the time to work through the process of dream, do, reflect? Do you discover anything that makes you want to evolve or do something different at your next meeting? Try repeating the same process with other meetings or events, such as parent meetings or professional learning events. What different questions might you ask yourself in any of the steps? Visioning is not a one-time event but rather an ever-evolving process.

"When I think of my experiences with a pedagogical leader, what comes to mind is a thinking partner. Someone who isn't afraid to nudge you in ways that speak to your strengths and pushes you further than you would have been able to go on your own. My experience with a pedagogical leader has been an adventurous one, one full of ups and downs, unexpected twists, realizations, celebrations, and growth, both personally and professionally. They have a way of bringing you into an unexpected journey, one that you never knew you wanted to go on or would go on but in the end you are excited to be a part of."

~ Jeanette, educator

When organizations have moved through the process of naming their values and building their vision grounded in these values, it provides both current and future employees with an understanding of the purpose of their collective work. When core values are identified, they offer insight to the identity of the organization and help people understand the shared values that drive behavior and decision-making. Where a clear vision provides direction and purpose, values provide a foundation for how all employees live together, make decisions, and spend their time and resources. Identifying the vision and values that guide your organization doesn't mean that everyone will immediately agree on everything. Having clarity is only the beginning, but it can offer pedagogical leaders and educators ongoing opportunities to consider and adopt practices that align with what they are trying to grow and the kind of people they want to be.

Several years ago, both London Bridge Child Care Services and Compass Early Learning and Care went through the formal process of identifying organizational core values. We say "identifying" them because, while there were many values that guided daily practice in both our organizations, a set of core values had not been named specifically. When we asked different people to articulate what they thought our core values were, there were many different ideas and interpretations. Not wanting to impose a new set of core values from the top down, we were more interested in exploring how values already lived within the organization and had already influenced decision-making.

Our initial process for identifying a set of core values was similar in both of our organizations.

1. Multiple small-group conversations took place across our organizations. Employees were asked to consider what values were important to them in their work, what kinds of things they cared most about, how they made decisions, and what values they believed already existed in the organization.
2. The ideas generated through small-group discussions and employee surveys were documented, revisited, and shared.
3. Organizational leaders found commonalities among employees' responses and used these to identify a set of core values that described how we saw ourselves living and acknowledged the kind of culture we wanted to grow.

This similar initial approach set both London Bridge and Compass on a path to eventually identify a set of organizational core values that grounded their vision and continue to guide our practice today. These values are at the core of our practice, yet they are ever evolving.

Naming our values out loud did not mean that we all started living in harmony together. In fact, identifying them specifically meant that we then had to continuously deconstruct what they look like in practice. It has been many years since we formally identified our company's core values, and yet we still find that living them requires continuous reflection and steadfast attention to opportunities for this work to happen. It requires patience, time, and pause. It calls us to offer time to listen to one another, consider different perspectives, grow in our own self-awareness, and deeply consider the intricacies of the things that we say are important to us. We also understand the great work that needs to be done in our organizations to bring the values of equity, diversity, and inclusion to the forefront of our work. As we are learning more together, we are exploring how these strong values can become more explicit and held in the deep regard we believe they require.

As pedagogical leaders, we have found that it is our core values and vision that guide us in decision-making. Rather than reacting on a whim or relying on a policy to make decisions for us, our values and vision can help ensure that the day-to-day decisions we make around how we spend time and money, access resources, or approach different situations align with the kind of community and people we want to be. Although living with a set of core values remains complex, we are learning that when we pause to reflect and consider these complexities together, we enable a more intentional practice.

PEDAGOGICAL LEADERS WORK TO ADVANCE EQUITY

Now consider . . .

What are the issues around equity that you think about in your work?

There is no doubt that there is much to be done to advance equity in early childhood. Systemic and deep-rooted inequities continue to advantage some over others, and child care programs are not exempt. It is the responsibility of all early learning professionals to take both the large and small steps needed to create a caring, equitable community for all children, educators, and families.

We admit that talking about equity issues is not easy. Just thinking about how we were going to address them in this book kept us both squirming for months. It's not that we are not deeply committed to it—we are. But in talking about issues of equity, we would be remiss if we didn't acknowledge that we are two white women who have contributed to and benefited from a system that has advantaged us disproportionately. We are on our own giant learning curve to understand the impact of our own actions and inheritances, and we have much to learn.

For us, advancing equity first and foremost requires humility, an openness to listen, and a willingness to study the impact of our own practice. As we continue to learn more about advancing equity in our own practice and lives, we turn for guidance to those with lived experience and who have been doing this work for years. We stumble, make mistakes, put our feet directly in our mouths, and then we get back to work. As we learn more about restorative justice, we try to turn our polite Canadian habit of saying

"I'm sorry" into action and making amends for our missteps. It's hard. Those common self-soothing phrases of "I didn't mean to" or "That was not my intention" no longer fly. Learning more about the impact of the decisions we make, the things we say, the policies we contribute to, and the actions we engage in is a lifelong commitment that we are all called to do in this field—and in society as a whole. We know that if we were to write this book a year from now, we would have greater insight to offer. Just as we know that if we had written it a year ago, we wouldn't be able to offer what we know today. That is the way it works. So today, as pedagogical leaders who are working to advance equity in our own work, here are the things that we think about.

Building Awareness

Recently in a discussion about antibias education, a colleague made a powerful comment: if you are not thinking about issues of equity, it means that you don't have to. What she meant was that for those who benefit from the system, learning about inequity and its effects on people is a choice, but people who face it every day have no choice.

Pedagogical leaders have a responsibility to help build awareness around systemic racism and issues of inequities and shine a light on the impact it has in our work. Building awareness is not a one-time process. Attending a workshop on cultural sensitivity may be a step, but it doesn't mean we are done. Awareness is an ongoing commitment to learning.

As individuals and as a community there is much for us to learn about the impact we have on each other. We have a responsibility to continue to grow awareness around the effect of things like the language we choose, our own history, and how privilege and power play out in our lives. Yet awareness alone can be a trickster. It can fool us into believing that thought is the same as action and that acknowledging is the same as repairing. Our work in helping to advance equity calls us to continuously learn about, notice, and respond to discrimination and unfairness as it plays out in its many forms, moment by moment.

Creating Intentional Learning Experiences

Talking about equity issues can elicit a wide range of emotion in people. Anger, guilt, defensiveness, withdrawal, confusion, sadness—even disbelief. When setting up learning opportunities, it is important to be clear about what your ground rules are. Here are some of the ground rules we have been offered by our colleagues Rukia Rogers, Sarah Felstiner, and Ijumaa Jordan that we have found useful.

Setting the Stage . . .

- Racism is real. No time will be spent discussing whether or not systemic racism and other forms of inequities really exist. They do!
- Racism and other forms of inequity happen in child care. Just because you might not see it doesn't mean it is not there.
- Prepare to be uncomfortable. There is a big difference between being unsafe and being uncomfortable. Acknowledging the difference can help prepare educators to enter into difficult conversations and hear difficult things.
- Prepare to not have closure. There are no quick fixes here.
- We are all good people who care deeply. Acknowledging our role in contributing to the problem is a key part in healing the system.

Some Things You Can Do . . .

- Access some of the many excellent books and resources that speak directly to equity and child care.
- Read the National Association for the Education of Young Children (NAEYC) Position Statement on Advancing Equity in Early Childhood Education.
- Look for opportunities to join online groups and webinars that are organized and led by people with lived experiences.
- Access videos, podcasts, documentaries, and articles and set up viewing evenings and discussion groups.
- Connect with Indigenous and other cultural communities near you.
- Learn about your history and the impact of settler colonialism.
- Amplify the voices of members of Black, Indigenous, and People of Color (BIPOC) communities. Intentionally offer resources from BIPOC authors, scholars, artists, and teachers to read, watch, and listen to.
- Learn about the Truth and Reconciliation Commission of Canada: Calls to Action.

- Audit your own resource library. Ensure that there is a wide representation of perspectives, experiences, and worldviews.
- Study and learn about antibias education and how to be an antibias teacher.
- Launch an organization-wide accounting of how white supremacy and inequity show up in who represents your leadership, your program policies, paperwork, distribution of resources, hiring practices, and paths to leadership.

"One of the most powerful things that our pedagogical leader has done for our center is to amplify voices that are not always heard. She offers us videos and podcasts that show diverse points of view and arranges time for us to have conversations about them. These experiences have enabled me to learn more about the different issues that I have been blinded to as a straight white person."

Luka, educator

When organizations, pedagogical leaders, and educators take the time to learn more about where inequity and bias come from and how they work, it starts to become easier to see how they show up in daily life. Listen to how pedagogical leader Renee reflects on her own practice to think about how language and equity play out in the classroom.

A new child had just joined the preschool classroom where Renee was working alongside two educators. Three-year-old Carlos knew a few words in English, but his first language, in which he was quite fluent, was Spanish. Between them, Renee and the educators could muster up a couple of words in Spanish but not enough to communicate with Carlos. At first, they caught themselves saying things like, "Sorry, I can't understand what you're telling me." Or they would smile and nod, saying things like, "OK, it's OK," or "Ahh, I see."

Renee found that these responses bothered her. She could feel a sense of discouragement in Carlos as he was trying to communicate something that they weren't understanding. She started to imagine what it must be like for him to be in a room all day where no one can communicate with him in his first language. As a pedagogical leader, Renee allowed herself to share her discomfort and offered up the thoughts and questions that were running through her own mind as a source for conversation. She began to wonder out loud what it does to a child to hear his educators constantly saying, "I'm sorry. I can't understand you." Is it Carlos's fault that we have a hard time understanding him? What does our behavior convey about the language that he can and does speak so effortlessly? What does it tell him about his family and their way of being and communicating with one another? How could we work harder to listen and understand this child, instead of insisting that he conform to a way of communicating that makes life easier for us?

As they began to take up these questions together, they noticed themselves saying things to Carlos like, "I'm sorry, I can't understand because I haven't learned enough Spanish yet," or "I'm going to try to learn more Spanish so that I can understand more of what you're sharing."

They started to make the uncomfortable realization of how often they had equated a child's ability to communicate with their ability to speak English. They realized that they seemed to be OK with letting children go misunderstood and had soothed themselves by saying things like, "They'll learn," meaning "They will learn English."

This acknowledgment led to new questions like, "When do we put the burden of adaptation on ourselves? What can we do to make our practices within the classroom more inclusive so that children like Carlos feel a greater sense of belonging? How do we also nurture a sense of belonging among our colleagues who are speaking English as a second, third, fourth, or fifth language? Where and when can we as English-only speakers make an effort to learn more about our colleagues? How can we create a working environment where we acknowledge and celebrate multiple languages?"

As the days passed Renee and the educators made a concerted effort to learn words and phrases in Spanish. Carlos seemed thrilled that the adults around him were trying to speak his language, and he started to teach them. He delighted and clapped for them as they practiced pronouncing the words he was teaching.

This back and forth continued, with Carlos teaching the educators Spanish and the educators teaching him English. All of them embarked together on a language-learning journey, trying to meet somewhere in the middle.

As a pedagogical leader, Renee is interested in gaining a better understanding of the cultural wealth that exists within the classrooms she works in. She sees it as her responsibility to continue to learn how bias and inequity show up in her own work and to acknowledge and disrupt the overrepresentation of white, Eurocentric ways of being in the classroom. She wants to encourage her organization to hire more educators who reflect the children and families they serve.

Pause and Reflect

How does Renee's experience make you think about your own equity work?

What comes to mind for you when you think of the cultural wealth that exists in your program or classroom?

When programs, pedagogical leaders, and educators take up the big work of learning about equity and systemic racism, they begin to shed light on the problematic histories and dominant narratives that have shaped the education system and their own organization. They start to focus a lens that they can use to examine their own policies and practices and build awareness around the impact that their decisions have on others.

Exploring Your Own Practice: Conducting a Book Audit

Getting good at studying ourselves, our programs, and our classroom or school communities to see where racism and bias show up is part of our collective work as early childhood professionals. One of the useful ways we found to help educators start to see just how much bias shows up in classrooms is to do a book audit. Every early childhood classroom has books, and books are not innocent. They can carry subtle, unintended messages that can be harmful. A hidden curriculum that is implicitly biased teaches unplanned lessons and values that undermine children's self-worth.

Use the following questions to learn more about how different biases might show up in your own classroom libraries.

www.redleafpress.org/crp/d-6.pdf

TITLE & AUTHOR OF BOOK: ______________________________

NAMES OF AUDITORS: ______________________________

DATE: ______________________________

Does the book carry any stereotypes?

A stereotype is an oversimplified generalization about a particular identity group (e.g., gender, race, ethnicity, class, sexual orientation, ability/disability), which usually carries derogatory, inaccurate messages and applies to all people in the group.

Who isn't represented? (acknowledging invisibility)

What children do not see in their books teaches them about who matters and who doesn't in our society. Look specifically for who and what is missing in your books. Consider things like race, culture, language, family structure, lifestyle, and ability.

Do you notice any tokenism?

Tokenism happens when a book has the appearance of being diverse but is still structured around a singular cultural ideal, in most cases white, middle-class, Eurocentric ideals. It is often revealed when there is only one of something. It could be a black or brown character that is swapped in for a white character or perhaps a character in a wheelchair who is added into the background for effect.

What are the messages about different lifestyles?

Do images and information in our books offer genuine insights into the lifestyles of the characters in the story? Do we have a wide range of diversity in our books, featuring characters of different cultures and heritage, showing a variety of life situations, and conveying accurate information about how different people live in the world?

How does this book portray human relationships with the earth?

Is the earth or are other nonhuman identities acknowledged or respected in any way? Or are they disregarded or portrayed as commodities to be used by humans?

After Auditing This Book . . .

- I am reconsidering . . .
- I would make a point to emphasize . . .
- I would balance it out by ensuring I have other stories that . . .
- I will continue to use this book but will reconsider how I offer it.
- This book is not appropriate for the children I work with.
- This book is not appropriate and delivers messages that concern me.

Adapted from SocialJusticeBooks.org

There is no one way for pedagogical leaders and educators to do this work. Advancing equity happens through building awareness; listening and learning from those with lived experiences; recognizing where bias exists in our classrooms, organizational structures, and policies; and then making organizational commitments to address them.

RECAPPING THE ROLE OF THE PEDAGOGICAL LEADER TO WORK FROM A PLACE OF VISION AND VALUES

Pedagogical leaders . . .

- Have a clear vision about the kind of learning community they want to build.
- Take time to dream about possibilities.
- Bring awareness around equity issues and notice and bring visibility to inequities.
- Create space to have courageous conversations around equity issues.
- Seek out a diverse collection of resources and amplify historically marginalized voices.
- Invite others to see past barriers and consider what they hope for themselves and for others.
- Ask specific questions to help ignite the imagination and generate new thinking.
- Notice and name small shifts in their own and in educators' attitudes and actions that have a desired impact.
- Have clarity around their own values.
- Help identify the values that are reflected in the physical environment, daily rituals, and relationships with the human and nonhuman world.
- Consider the values that drive how they respond and encourage others to identify the values that influence their responses.
- Notice when there are conflicting values at play and help educators consider different points of view.
- Notice when their actions are misaligned with their values and work to repair relationships.
- Advocate that the organization creates systems and structures to advance equity and uphold values.

CHAPTER THREE

Pedagogical Leaders Focus on Building Meaningful Relationships

"Trust is the glue of life. It's the most essential ingredient in effective communication. It's the foundational principle that holds all relationships."

Steven R. Covey

Take a moment to consider:

What words come to mind for you when you think about the close relationships in your life?

How do you feel when you are with these people?

What do you believe are the characteristics of close, trusting relationships?

Any early childhood educator can tell you that building caring and nurturing relationships with children is one of the most important things they do. When children form strong emotional attachments to others, they feel safe to experiment with ideas and engage in complex play. They experience a greater sense of belonging and are able to contribute and connect to others. When children are with adults they trust, they begin to develop the footing they need to confront challenges, express ideas, and discover more about themselves and the world around them. In short, learning happens best when children are with people they care about and who care about them. What we have come to know is that strong, positive relationships hold a learning community together and are what enable a pedagogical leader to work successfully within all the other pedagogical leadership principles.

Meaningful relationships are also an integral part of learning for adults. Pedagogical leaders understand this and work to foster strong and trusting relationships among children and adults alike. They intentionally develop approaches that nurture the kind of relationships with educators that they hope educators will nurture with children. We think of this paralleling of practice as the golden rule of pedagogical leadership.

While building meaningful relationships might come easier with some than with others, it can be helpful to understand that we are not talking about the kind of relationships built solely on social niceties or ones that require individuals to become best friends. Instead, we are talking about the kind of relationships that enable educators to bring their authentic selves to their work. These relationships are built on trust, mutual respect, care, concern, and a deep desire to support each other. These relationships require intentionally planned experiences, processes, and approaches that provide for sharing multiple perspectives, ideas, and practices. Like children, when educators feel safe and secure, they are more likely to take risks, share their thinking, try something new, or offer a different perspective. When educators can trust that a pedagogical leader is genuinely interested in what they have to say, there is a stronger likelihood that they will share their ideas openly. When they feel heard, they are often more willing to dig into their own thinking by exploring both what they think and why they think it. When educators feel that what they have to say is valid and worthy of being heard, they are more likely to listen to children's ideas with the same deep regard. When they feel supported with a transparent structure to engage in this vulnerable work, they are more likely to fully participate with others.

One of the most important aspects of a pedagogical leader's role is to get to know the people they work with. Who are they? What do they care about? What challenges or excites them? What are their strengths, and how do they learn best? Every person brings their own complex story, way of being, individual identity, culture and family background, history, and experience to their work. Pedagogical leaders understand that embracing the uniqueness of individuals and rejecting the idea of sameness is an important step in creating respectful relationships among a community of learners. Planning specific ways to help this happen will ensure individuals will more easily feel safe and a sense of belonging.

Strong, trusting relationships lead to a deeper level of engagement, enabling both educators and pedagogical leaders to question ideas together. Trust allows for differences to exist while still working toward a shared vision. This enables groups of people to resist trying to find one right answer but rather to explore and experiment with different possibilities. When pedagogical leaders and educators are in a relationship with each other, they find it easier to see themselves as co-learners. Guided by a shared vision and values, they learn to engage with each other's curiosity and interests. Coworkers become resources for each other, and educators are active participants in their own learning. Pedagogical leaders can design questions and experiences that consistently include these various ways to grow trusting, useful relationships for reflective practice.

It is for these same reasons that pedagogical leaders encourage and support educators in nurturing relationships with families and their wider communities. Children live in a world that is larger than their own classrooms. They are influenced by multiple relationships, the most important being with their own family. When close bonds strengthen partnerships between educators and their students' families, adults can safely share concerns, perspectives, values, and worldviews. It is clear that trusting relationships contribute to health and well-being and are paramount to both child and adult learning.

The kinds of relationships we have can and should reach beyond human to human. We are at a critical time in history when human activity has significantly affected Earth, the home we are leaving to our children. Pedagogical leaders work with educators to consider the kinds of relationships we build with the nonhuman world and the environmental impact of our practices.

The importance of nurturing strong relationships cannot be understated. Relationships are the glue that holds a learning community together and enable a pedagogical leader to work successfully with each of the principles we've identified in this book. Yet building these kinds of relationships doesn't just happen. It requires intentionality.

We have found the following to be important ways that pedagogical leaders can build strong relationships with educators, children, families, and the Earth that sustains us. These are not simply strategies but instead ways of being that, when lived consistently and over time, can evolve practice and create a sense of well-being for a whole learning community.

Pedagogical leaders . . .

1. Nurture the kinds of relationships with educators they hope educators nurture with children.
2. Intentionally facilitate strong relationships among groups.
3. Strengthen relationships by listening.
4. Focus on building meaningful relationships with families and communities.
5. Help grow relationships between the human and nonhuman world.

PEDAGOGICAL LEADERS NURTURE THE KINDS OF RELATIONSHIPS WITH EDUCATORS THEY HOPE EDUCATORS NURTURE WITH CHILDREN

Now consider . . .

How do you nurture relationships with others?

How have your relationships with others influenced your practice?

What can happen when pedagogical leaders approach their work with educators with the same deep regard they want educators to have for children? The golden rule of pedagogical leadership explores the idea of creating a paralleled practice between pedagogical leaders and educators and educators and children. It is based on the notion that the values and experiences that are important for children are also important for adults.

Consider for a moment the kinds of things you want for children. How do you want them to feel when they are at the center? How do you want them to be treated? What kinds of things do you think about when you consider their well-being? Now consider these same questions as you think about what you want for educators, families, and even yourself. While the specific experiences may look different for everyone, the desire we all have to feel a sense of belonging, to express ourselves and be heard, to have opportunities to engage in meaningful ways, and to feel safe are human experiences we all deserve.

"Parallel practice reminds me of the oneness of humanity. When we recognize that what is often true in our practice with young children is also true in our lives with everyone else we encounter, we can move away from 'othering' and see ourselves in the world around us. For example, when I understand that the joy and intrigue of open-ended materials is universal, I see the significance of these opportunities in the classroom more clearly.

"Something I have noticed to be most important in my understanding of parallel practice is to question my assumptions and unconscious decisions in my work. For example, I may decide it is important to pay attention to the competencies in children but may unconsciously not take the time to notice the competencies of my colleagues. Whatever the reason for this unconscious disconnect, when I pause, reflect, and notice this discrepancy, only then am I able to move into alignment."

Mary, pedagogical leader

Pedagogical leaders recognize the connection between their work with educators and educators' work with children and consciously find ways to parallel their practice. The golden rule invites pedagogical leaders to think about the kind of culture they want to nurture and what that can look like for children and adults alike. Paralleling practice can offer educators an opportunity to experience for themselves something that they in turn can offer children. It disrupts the hypocrisy that can exist when educators are treated one way but are expected to treat children a different way. Notice how pedagogical leader Amanda uses paralleling to offer an educator a different experience to consider her work.

Over the course of three to four weeks, there had been some concerning changes happening in the preschool classroom. Three educators had left, giving various reasons for their departure, and the classroom had a constant flow of substitute educators. More and more children were yelling or crying, and parent complaints were at an all-time high.

When the center's pedagogical leader, Amanda, visited the classroom, she noticed that toys and loose materials were scattered all over the room. She saw children grabbing things out of each other's hands and being aggressive. She watched as the children wandered from one area in the classroom to another, not appearing to focus on or engage in any particular thing. She noticed children trying to get the attention of the educators before they climbed up onto tables. She also noticed that the newest educator in the room, Sarah, was clearly frustrated.

Amanda could see that classroom support was clearly needed and arranged a meeting with Sarah. Sarah came to the meeting prepared with her notes and a comprehensive plan for "fixing the problem." As Amanda listened, she could see that Sarah's solutions fell into three common reactions:

1. Remove or manage the problem: taking toys and denying children certain experiences.
2. Create rules: giving children lists of things they were not allowed to do.
3. Impose consequences: using a punitive approach when children broke the rules.

Pause and Reflect

Do these responses feel familiar to you?

What are some common reactions you notice to challenging situations in the classroom?

How might you respond to a similar situation?

Amanda recognized that Sarah was trying to fix a problem before she understood what was causing the problem in the first place. Through their conversations she could see that Sarah wanted to be recognized as a competent educator and that she believed the behavior of the children was a reflection on her. Sarah's strong desire to change what was happening in the classroom led her to suggest an enforcement approach.

As a pedagogical leader, Amanda encouraged Sarah to consider not just what the children were doing but why they were doing it. As they continued to talk more about what was happening in the classroom, Amanda could see Sarah's frustration growing. It seemed clear to Amanda that Sarah defaulted to an enforcement approach because she didn't know what else to do.

Instead of offering solutions as a pedagogical leader, Amanda supported Sarah by refocusing the conversation around what they wanted for the children and expressed her own curiosity about what might be happening. She offered to spend a couple of days in the classroom with Sarah to see if together they could develop some theories about what might be going on.

Amanda designed some questions that could provide a lens for them to observe the children together.

What do we think the children are trying to do?

What are they showing us about what they know?

What kinds of things are they struggling with?

How does the environment affect what might be happening here?

Pause and Reflect

How do you think these questions might nurture curiosity in the educator?

How does observing from a place of curiosity change the way we respond to a challenging situation?

After spending a couple of days together in the classroom, they came up with some theories about what the children might be communicating through their actions.

- "Notice me": "I want to engage with you and am willing to do what it takes to get your attention."
- "I want to play": "I see what you are doing and I want to do it too."
- "I'm afraid to share": "If I give you what I have, then I won't be able to play."
- "I have too many choices; I feel overwhelmed."

As the two fleshed out their theories together, Sarah developed a different perspective for her decision-making. Her response to the children began to change. Instead of imposing rules, she acknowledged what she thought they were trying to do and helped them find respectful ways to do it. Just as her pedagogical leader worked side by side in the classroom with her, Sarah began to work side by side with the children.

Just as her pedagogical leader designed careful questions for Sarah as opposed to solutions, Sarah did the same with the children. Sarah began by ensuring that each child felt listened to. She created specific spaces in the classroom where children could play on their own, and instead of leaving out buckets of loose parts, she started to create intrigue by staging them and engaging children in conversations. Sarah slowly reshaped the relationship dynamic she had with the children. They could see that she cared about their ideas and began to trust her.

With the help of her pedagogical leader, Sarah's original solution of removing or managing the problem, creating rules, and imposing consequences shifted to assisting, coaching, facilitating, and rearranging. This story is a good example of how strong, trusting relationships can grow from everyday practice. When educators have a pedagogical leader who cares about them and their success and who designs questions and approaches that call on their thinking, they are more open to considering the implications of their own practice. Having a trusted mentor with whom they can think through real-life challenges can help educators resist the temptation to try to fix problems before really understanding them. When educators have a strong relationship with a pedagogical leader, they are more apt to try new approaches, test new theories, and become more curious about their own thinking without fear of not being right. Pedagogical leaders can purposefully help educators intentionally learn from their own experiences.

"When I think about the power of relationships, I think about how the connection I have with myself, co-educators, and the children all intertwine. One cannot thrive without the others also thriving. This belief is what strengthens me personally, professionally, and pedagogically."

Priscilla, educator

Exploring Your Own Practice: Paralleling Practice

Working on your own or with others, consider some specific ways that pedagogical leaders and educators can use this kind of parallel thinking to consider how they might build strong relationships. What are your thoughts about these ideas? What other ideas can you add?

Ways to Build Trusting Relationships	• How pedagogical leaders do this for educators and educators do this for children
Get to know others as individuals.	• Pay attention to the things educators and children talk about. Notice what kinds of things they get excited about. What motivates or inspires them? • What other things might you do to get to know educators?
Build trust.	• To build trust, it is important that you are honest and trustworthy. Show trust in the educators and children, and follow through with what you say you will do. • What other specific ways might you build trust with educators and children?
Focus on strengths.	• How might you offer educators and children opportunities to contribute to the life of the center in ways that draw on their individual interests, skills, or talents? • What specific ways might you highlight the strengths of educators and children?
Provide opportunities for ideas to be heard.	• When might you provide educators and children opportunities to express different viewpoints? • How do you encourage educators and children to listen to each other? • How do you encourage and respect ideas that may be different? • What specific ways might you provide opportunities for educators and children to feel heard?

PEDAGOGICAL LEADERS INTENTIONALLY FACILITATE STRONG RELATIONSHIPS AMONG GROUPS

Now consider . . .

How do you build trust with the people you work with?

What intentional practices have you found most useful?

In Ontario in 2014, the Ministry of Education released a new pedagogy for the early years titled *How Does Learning Happen? Ontario's Pedagogy for the Early Years* (Ontario Public Service). It was created as a resource for the early learning sector in an effort to promote a shared understanding of what children need to grow and flourish. Bravely, it was not a checklist or rating scale but rather a tool for reflection with emphasis on the critical importance of positive relationships to learning. Ontario is certainly not alone in this thinking. More and more early learning frameworks from around the world are exploring the notion that learning happens in relationships. If we want to create an environment where learning can grow and flourish, we must create an environment and specific tools that foster positive, trusting relationships.

> *"I instantly think about the power of being in relationship. When we are in relationship, we can create and share stories, we can collaborate and build on ideas, we can challenge and support one another, and we can grow. Being in relationship builds community. Being in relationship holds us up and invites us to bring our true and authentic selves to the table."*
>
> *Shelley, educator*

As we continue to explore how we construct and co-construct knowledge together, our roles are evolving. Educators are reimagining the kind of environment that truly sets the scene for learning. As educators are reconsidering this for children, the role of the pedagogical leader is to also create intentional practices that support the building and growing of relationships among teams. Relationship building takes time, and in an already busy program, it can feel like it takes away from our work alongside children. When we see this practice as serving on behalf of children and each other, we are more likely to find ways to carve out time.

September is often a busy month in early learning programs. Children transition from one class to another. New children start while others leave, and new educator teams are forming. These new team dynamics are much like arranged marriages, often chosen with the belief that as they get to know one another, the relationship will naturally develop. While this may be true for some, for many these new partnerships can be tricky. Pedagogical leaders understand the importance of offering time and space for educator teams to share their hopes and dreams for their program. When they are given an opportunity to share their values and express what they need from one another, they gain a deeper understanding of each other. The same can be true for different groups of children. Consider this story of how pedagogical leader Ryan creates intentional practices for building relationships and how this parallel works with children and among children.

As an experienced pedagogical leader, Ryan had come to understand that taking the time to meet with new teams of educators within the first couple of weeks of their partnership helps to get these marriages off on the right foot. While there are always many things that need to be done, Ryan made it a priority to bring teams together to facilitate a conversation that can help educators jointly think about what they want for themselves and their classrooms.

He developed questions to help guide their discussion:

How do we want children to feel in our classroom? How do we want to feel?

What is the culture we are trying to create?

What do we need from one another to grow a sense of trust?

Once the teams have a chance to reflect together about these questions, Ryan helps educators generate a list of agreements that helps to guide them in their work moving forward. Here is an example of one of the classrooms' initial agreements:

Our Agreements

- Be open to different ideas and perspectives.
- Respect each other.
- Have open communication.
- Follow through on commitments.
- Be honest.

Understanding that the list is only a starting point, Ryan helped teams clarify their agreements and bring visibility to their thinking. He led discussions about what key words and ideas mean to them individually. For example, this preschool team agreed that respecting each other was a strong value they wanted to bring to their work. Ryan invited each team to dig deeper by offering the following questions:

What does respect look like in our work together as a team?

What does respect look like in our work with children and with families?

What kinds of things will we see happening when we respect each other?

Pause and Reflect

What do you notice about the different ways people think about common words or ideas?

What helps you learn more about others' perspectives?

The act of digging deeper into agreements allowed time for each of the teams to fill out their own ideas as well as listen to others. The result was a fuller list of agreements.

Our Agreements

- Be open to different ideas and perspectives.
- Different perspectives broaden your mind.
- Be willing to try to see the other person's point of view.
- Try new things.
- Be willing to take a risk and possibly fail.
- Respect each other.
- Be willing to accept and work with differences.
- Don't turn other's ideas down; build on them.
- Believe that we are all doing the best that we can.
- Listen with curiosity.
- Have open communication.
- Be honest and kind to one another.
- Understand that we all want the best for each other and children.
- Talk to each other when there is a problem.
- Support each other.
- Help each other to articulate and try ideas.
- Be willing to learn from each other.
- Pause and help each other when needed.
- Help each other to notice when you are stopping children's activities or actions. Then, step back and see what will happen.
- Follow through on commitments.
- Each person is responsible to take ownership of the classroom.
- Ask for support when you need it.
- Be open and prepared to share.
- Bring observations, notes, photographs, and all other meaningful data to meetings.

Over the weeks and months there was a palpable shift in the classrooms, among the teams, and with the children. Because of their shared agreements, educators showed a willingness to listen to each other, trusting that each person on the team was focusing on what they were trying to build together. They began to notice small positive shifts in the relationships between children and themselves.

Pause and Reflect

What kinds of agreements have you considered in your work with others?

How do you create time and space for teams to come together to create shared agreements?

Agreements are effective, but unless they become an embedded intentional part of practice, they can go away as easily as they came. Pedagogical leaders help keep agreements relevant by revisiting and reflecting on them often.

"As a pedagogical leader I have found that taking the time to talk about and set agreements about how we want to be and behave together, prior to starting our work, supports the group in times when emotions can run high. Writing down what it is we all agree to gives us something tangible to review when we need to pause and ground ourselves. Revisiting them regularly ensures their relevancy and provides an opportunity to add to them when moments arise that we hadn't considered initially."

Angela, pedagogical leader

Here are some questions that Ryan used to help educators revisit the agreements they made together.

What are you noticing about how agreements are working in your classroom?

What are you learning about yourself and each other?

How are these agreements moving you toward the goal and vision you have for your classroom?

Do any of the agreements need more clarity? Do we need to add any to the list?

The act of making agreements also builds relationships, helping educators understand one another. When educators see the value and power of collective thinking and collaboration in making agreements, they can move toward this in the classroom with the children. When pedagogical leaders encourage setting agreements as a consistent practice in forming new relationships and communities, making and reflecting on agreements becomes a part of practice in programs.

New teams often form at the same time new children come together. In classrooms, especially those with preschool and school-age children, educators often post a list of classroom rules or agreements. However, these are commonly created by educators for the children. The list often includes listening to each other and the educator, respecting each other, keeping hands to yourself, etc. The intention of the educator is to create a safe, equitable, and productive learning environment.

This had been true in the school-age program in this same center. The team had a traditional approach at the beginning of each year to post the classroom rules, going over them with the children and taking notice when children were not following the rules. It was always a struggle, and they spent more time policing the rules than they did engaging in relationships with the children. After this team had the opportunity to make their own agreements together with support of their pedagogical leader, their practice with children shifted.

Using the same process that teams had gone through, educators invited children to talk together about making agreements for their classroom. The agreements the children created were richer, more collaborative, and more thoughtful than the rules the teachers had listed. The robust conversation among the children also deepened the educators' understanding of the children, what they cared about, and how deeply they understood relationships.

In the weeks ahead, the educators witnessed children listening to each other more, inviting each other into play, and reminding each other of their agreements when things got off track. The educators' image of the children also shifted, and they noted that they had a deeper understanding of the competencies of children. When pedagogical leaders hold educators in the same deep regard they want educators to hold for children, we see a shift in practice.

Pause and Reflect

What do you notice about how agreements can influence relationships between educators and children?

What does this story have you thinking about now in your practice?

In a school-age classroom, the educators witnessed how children used this same idea to advocate for themselves. The outdoor space in this program was vast and lined with beautiful shade trees, the kind of trees that were made for climbing. Unfortunately, the school prohibited climbing on the trees during school hours for perceived safety reasons. The children longed to climb the trees after school. The educators, who held a strong value for this kind of play, allowed the children to climb the trees after school hours. This, however, was frowned upon by the teachers in the school, and they often came out to the yard asking the children to get down. The educators continued to advocate for climbing, but the response from the school was clear: "It is not safe for the children to climb. They are too young, and someone will get hurt."

Believing in the strong relationships that had been built and witnessing the children's competencies to negotiate and listen to one another, they invited the children to create a list of agreements around how they would climb the trees safely. The children proposed these guidelines to the school in hopes of being permitted to climb the trees.

We agree:

- Ask an educator before you climb.
- Never climb on a branch smaller than your wrist.
- Don't step on branches that are broken, and if you hear a crack, get off.
- No picking leaves off the trees.
- If you can't get up the tree, then you probably can't get down, so no going up.

It was clear that the children had thought carefully about safety, caring for the tree as a living thing, and communicating their ideas. They presented these ideas to families and the school and were allowed to climb the trees after school using the guidelines they had created.

As you can see, the role of the pedagogical leader in providing time, space, and planned questions for teams to communicate and develop agreements can lead to a parallel in practice with children and among children.

Exploring Your Own Practice: Forming and Reflecting on Agreements

Practice making agreements at your next staff meeting. Invite the group to consider:

- How do we want children to feel in our program? How do we want to feel?
- What is the culture we are trying to create?
- What do we need from one another to grow a sense of trust?

Take some time to fill out the groups' ideas and consider the behavior and practices that align with what you are trying to grow. Be sure to check in during future staff meetings and consider:

- What are we noticing about how agreements are working in the program?
- What are we learning about ourselves and others?
- How are these agreements moving us toward our goals and vision for the program?
- Do any of the agreements need more clarity? Are there new ones we need to add to the list?

PEDAGOGICAL LEADERS STRENGTHEN RELATIONSHIPS BY LISTENING

Now consider . . .

How do you feel when someone really listens to you?

What practices do you follow to help you suspend judgment and focus on listening?

When we learn to listen well, we begin to learn more about each other's lives. This is especially important as we engage more in real conversations about race, inclusion, fairness, and justice. The reality is that these conversations are not easy or comfortable. They require self-awareness, a lowering of defensiveness, and a willingness to listen with openness and humility.

> *"During a debriefing session, thought-provoking questions made me feel uncomfortable at first, but later I learned that it was OK to feel discomfort and uncertainty."*
>
> ∾ *Sonya, educator*

In our work and travels we frequently ask educators to talk about those leaders who have truly inspired them. When they share the qualities of these leaders, they often recount stories or times when they really felt heard and knew that their ideas were valued and appreciated. They talk about feeling safe and understanding that these leaders truly care about them and have an investment in their learning. They truly want to know what they think and why they think it, free of judgment.

See if you recognize the way you listen in any of the following:

Pretend Listening Do you ever start thinking about what you have to pick up on the way home or mentally start preparing for your next meeting?	Pretend listeners are often distracted by their own thoughts, and while they maintain eye contact and lean in, they really aren't listening at all.
Selective Listening Do you find that when you're trying to listen you become easily distracted until a word or sentence that you connect with draws you in?	Selective listeners often see or hear only what they want to hear, tuning out others' ideas or perspectives.
Listening to Respond Do you start thinking of a story you have about the same idea? Do you think about how you are going to "fix" their problem or give advice?	This is the level that we most frequently use when listening. It often comes from our passions and deep desire to help others and give advice. When we listen to respond, we can't truly listen because we are often busy thinking about what we are going to say next.
Listening with Judgment I can't believe they think like that!	This level of listening is detrimental when trying to build relationships with others. When someone feels judged, they likely feel distrusted, shut down, and undervalued. When people feel judged, trust is lost.
Empathetic Listening I wonder why they believe that?	Listening with real curiosity requires that we be fully present, interested in understanding, and open to hearing others' ideas, perspectives, and opinions.

Adapted from Stephen R. Covey, *The Seven Habits of Highly Effective People: Restoring the Character Ethic.* New York: Simon and Schuster, © 1989.

In his world-renowned book *The Seven Habits of Highly Effective People,* Stephen Covey suggests empathetic listening, or listening to understand, is the highest form of listening. As pedagogical leaders, we would add another type of listening to that list: generative listening. Generative listening happens when people purposely listen for ideas and thoughts they can build on together. From empathetic listening it grows to generate the kinds of new thinking and collaborative understandings that are central to effective group work.

Listening is a key interpersonal skill, and by learning to listen more effectively, pedagogical leaders can improve the quality of their relationships and effectiveness with others. When pedagogical leaders listen with deep curiosity, they ask the questions to provoke educators' thinking and help them articulate their own ideas. Listen to the dialogue between a pedagogical leader and educator as the pedagogical leader leans in and listens with curiosity.

A frustrated educator complained to her pedagogical leader that her teammate was not "pulling their weight." She explained that they had discussed dividing the work in the classroom, but she felt like she was doing everything and constantly redoing the things that her coworker didn't follow through with.

Educator: I'm so frustrated! We divided up the daily tasks in our room, and we agreed upon it, but Jessica isn't following through. I feel like I have to do everything now, and it isn't fair to me!

Pedagogical leader: You do sound frustrated. Can you tell me more about dividing the tasks?

Educator: We both agreed that she would create identity panels and update them when new children start. Two new children still don't have them up and it looks bad on me, so I went ahead and did them. Now she is angry with me for taking over. But I had no choice because they needed to get done. She doesn't even care that they didn't get done.

Pedagogical leader: Help me understand what you mean when you say "I had no choice."

Educator: Well, I didn't. They weren't done, and families and children deserve them, and I had to do it.

Pedagogical leader: Do you think that Jessica also believes that they deserve them?

Educator: Well, if she does, I don't see it. She was doing them before, but she is falling behind and it looks bad on me.

Pedagogical leader: So, she was doing them before and has stopped? Why do you think that is?

Educator: I don't know; she was doing them before. Maybe she doesn't see it as important anymore.

Pedagogical leader: Is it important?

Educator: Yes! Children deserve to see themselves as part of the group. Their identity panel is one way we do that. Families also deserve to see the stories of what is happening in our classroom every day. They love getting them.

Pedagogical leader: You seem to be assuming that she doesn't see the value in these anymore. Is there anything that has happened aside from this that makes you believe that is true?

Educator: No, not really, just this. But when she didn't get to it, she got angry that I did it.

Pedagogical leader: Why do you think she might be upset about that?

Educator: I don't know. Maybe because I didn't talk to her about it first.

Pedagogical leader: So, it sounds like you will talk to her first the next time.

Educator: Yeah, well, maybe I could ask her why she isn't getting the panels done and if she doesn't really think they are that important. I suppose I could offer to take these tasks if she can't get to them.

Pedagogical leader: It sounds like you have a plan. You're going to connect with Jessica and find out if she needs any support and what you might do to help at this time.

Educator: Yes, and maybe we can also talk about the values we have for this work again. Maybe we can look again at how we are dividing things and see if it still works.

Pedagogical leader: Sounds like you have a way forward.

"In the twenty-five-year span of my career, I have been privileged to have a handful of people who I consider my mentors. These individuals are experts at listening to what I want, then offering me what I need. And more often than not, what they offer back to me is not overly profound or complex. Rather, what they offer me is often something quite simple yet powerful—and that is the magic little morsel that propels my thinking to the next level."

~ Shelley, educator

Pause and Reflect

How does the pedagogical leader use questions to move the conversation?

How is this similar to or different from your conversations with educators?

Questions can be a powerful tool for pedagogical leaders. They can help to clarify and probe different opinions and viewpoints and deepen educators' practice and thinking. Using questions as an approach to listening stimulates critical thinking and problem-solving and can be a way to illuminate ideas. It helps educators better understand what they already know. Questions drive our practice, not answers.

The oldest and most powerful teaching strategy for fostering critical thinking was offered to us more than twenty-five hundred years ago by Greek philosopher Socrates. Socrates developed a theory of knowledge based on asking and answering questions to stimulate critical thinking. This disciplined method of inquiry has come to be known as Socratic questioning. In our work, we have found that studying how Socrates used questions has helped us reflect on the quality and intention of our own questions. Socratic questions fall into six categories. Here are a few examples of different types of questions.

Questions That Help Clarify **Purpose:** To get people to think more about exactly what they are asking or thinking about. **Method:** Use basic "tell me more" questions that get them to go deeper.	• Can you give me an example? • Can you say that in a different way? • How does this relate to what we are talking about? • What exactly does that mean? • What do we already know about this? • What do you mean by ________? • What is your main point? • Elena, can you summarize what you think Arju said? Arju, did she get it right? • Can you say more about that?
Questions That Probe Assumptions **Purpose:** To help people to think more about why they believe what they do and what they are basing their views on.	• Explain why you feel this way. • You seem to be assuming ________. What else could we assume? • What is Nash assuming here? • Does anyone have a different assumption?

Questions That Seek Reason and Evidence **Purpose:** To dig into a reason for assumptions or arguments given. People often use unexamined ideas or weak reasoning to support their arguments.	• Can you give me an example of that? • What do you think causes ________? • Why do you think that is true? • What are your reasons for saying that? Are these reasons good enough? • What other information would be helpful to have here? • What evidence is there to support what you are saying? • Who is in a position to know if this is true? • Where could we get more information on this?
Questions about Opinions or Viewpoints **Purpose:** To explore other equally valid viewpoints. These can come from others in the group or be offered by the facilitator.	• What alternative ways might we look at this? • Who benefits from this? • Why is this better than ________? • How are what you and Cassandra are saying similar? • Another way to think about this is ________; does that make sense to you? • What would a child (family, coworkers, licenser, etc.) think? • How might you respond to ________? • Who says (something different)?
Questions That Imply Implications and Consequences **Purpose:** To consider logical implications of what people are saying and to consider if these make sense or are desirable.	• Then what would happen? • How does ________ affect ________? • How does what you are saying link with what we want for children, families, each other?
Questions about the Question **Purpose:** To consider the quality of the question itself.	• What was the purpose or point of that question? • How else might I ask this question? • Can we break this question down at all? • Is the question clear? • Is the question easy or hard to answer? Why? • Why is this question important? • Does this question lead to other questions or issues?

Pedagogical leaders can use these questions to support educators in exploring complex ideas, uncover their own assumptions, and bring to light new and innovative ways of thinking. Revisit the dialogue between the pedagogical leader and educator. Can you identify how the pedagogical leader used Socratic questions as a way of listening?

Exploring Your Own Practice: Practice Listening

During a team meeting or staff meeting, work in small groups of three or four to practice listening. Choose one person to be the speaker and one person the listener; the rest act as observers. Invite the speaker to consider a complex or challenging issue they are dealing with and are willing to speak about. The role of the listener is to listen from a place of curiosity and seek to understand the speaker, using questions to help the speaker fill out their own ideas and work through their challenge. The role of the observers is to listen and notice how the dialogue evolves. After the exercise the group can debrief and consider the following:

Listeners

- What did you notice about yourself in this exercise?
- What strategies were helpful in deepening your understanding of what the speaker was saying?
- Did you feel like you wanted to solve the person's challenge?

Speakers

- Did you feel like you were heard? Explain.
- Did you feel as though people tried to solve your problem?
- Did you come to think any differently about your challenge?
- Was talking through your challenge in this way helpful to you?

Observers

- What did you notice happening between the listener and speaker?
- What specific strategies did you notice the listener using to understand the speaker?
- What does this exercise have you thinking about your own listening practice?

PEDAGOGICAL LEADERS FOCUS ON BUILDING MEANINGFUL RELATIONSHIPS WITH FAMILIES AND COMMUNITIES

Now consider . . .

How do you welcome families and children into your care?

What does it really mean to have partnerships with families?

The decision to place a child into the care of someone else is a highly emotional one for families. When parents are considering child care options, they often put their children on waiting lists for early learning programs as soon as they find out they are expecting. The financial pressure combined with the emotional stress of leaving their child with someone else can be difficult for families. Pedagogical leaders play an important role in helping educators welcome families and children into their program. With some thoughtful planning, together pedagogical leaders and educators can ensure that relationships start off right and stay strong throughout the time children are in care. Listen to the story of ten-month-old Julia and her family as they began their journey in an early learning program.

Julia's parents had toured several different child care programs when they first found out they were expecting. They were in search of a place where they knew their child would be safe and well cared for and that would best fit with their family's values. When they came to the early learning center, they knew it was the right place for them. When they arrived, they were warmly welcomed by Diane, the center's pedagogical leader. Where other center tours had seemed focused solely on giving out information that highlighted daily schedules, routines, ratios, payment options, and licensing criteria, they could see that this program was also interested in learning more about who they were as a family and how their family values connected with the program. Diane eagerly shared the foundational values of the program and how they were present in the environments and practices.

As they began their tour through the center, they noticed photos of all of the educators, with little stories about who they were and what room they worked in. The center's value statements were prominently displayed alongside photos from the program, showing the values in practice. Diane walked Julia and her family through the center, highlighting pieces of documentation that showed how the educators used images and stories to bring attention to children's competencies.

There were four classrooms, each one unique, bright, uncluttered, and rich with materials and experiences for children. Small groups of children from each room were inside, while others were outside. Diane explained how the educators in each classroom divided the children into primary care groups to allow for smaller group experiences and a different kind of connection with each child. When they arrived at the infant room where Julia would be placed, Diane introduced Julia and her family to their primary caregiver, Jessica. She then took over for Jessica in the classroom so that Jessica could take over the tour and spend some time getting to know Julia's family. By the time the tour ended, Julia's family knew this was the right place for them.

In the days leading up to her first day, Julia's parents received a short form to fill out. This "introducing your child" sheet was a way to get to know Julia better. The form included questions about eating and sleeping habits and also invited Julia's parents to share more about their family's values and traditions and the hopes and dreams they had for their child.

Diane created time and space for Julia's new educators to meet together to review the form and reflect on the best ways to welcome Julia on her first day. When her parents arrived, a picture they had taken during her visit was used to identify where her belongings went. There was a portfolio on the shelf next to her cubby. Inside was an image of primary caregiver Jessica with a lovely welcome message.

After a few tears and a goodbye, Julia's parents went off to work. In her first few days at the center, Julia's parents received images and stories of her time in the program, and at the end of the week, they were invited to take Julia's portfolio home so they could revisit stories and experiences from her first week. A photo of Julia was placed on the wall alongside those of the other children in the classroom, which included captions underneath with the hopes and dreams that the families shared that first day. Pedagogical leaders understand the importance of these first visits and first days within a program and support practices that allow educators time and space to foster these.

Pause and Reflect

How do you get to know new families?

What values and practices do you make visible when you offer tours to new and prospective families?

As educators and pedagogical leaders, we want to honor the social, cultural, and linguistic diversity of our families. How we welcome each individual family into our program sets a tone for the authentic relationships to grow right from the start. These questions can act as a way to open dialogue around the considerations we want to think about in the first days and weeks in our programs. They can help us build structures throughout our programs and organization for this most important work of welcoming families.

Preparing for a New Child's Arrival

- What opportunities will there be for families and children to engage in the program before they start?
- How might families share their personal cultural stories?
- What strategies might you think about to show value to families' first language?
- How might you create ways for families within the program to connect?
- What provisions are made for children's belongings for their first day? What might you do to make this most welcoming?
- What structures are in place to share stories and experiences from the classroom? How have you discovered families' unique communication needs?

In a Child's First Few Days

- How will you make connections with families in their first days? What consideration might you make for a family's language or access to technology?
- How will you document and share experiences with families in these first days?
- Are the family and child visible throughout the classroom?

Before a Child Transitions to a New Classroom

- How will you engage family in the transition plan for their child?
- What individual needs are considered when planning visits?
- Has a place for their belongings been identified in the new environment?
- Who will be the child's new educator(s)? Have there been opportunities to introduce the educator(s) and family before the transition?
- How will the history of the child's experiences be shared or move with the child into their new classroom?

In the Child's First Few Days in Their New Classroom

- What communication plan do you have for the first days in the program? How will you document and share experiences with families in these first days?
- Are the family and child visible throughout the classroom?

Carefully setting the stage from the start allows relationships with children and their families to grow. The pedagogical leader can work with educators to ensure that thoughtful practices welcome and transition new children and families to their programs. Transitioning from one classroom to another is a milestone for most children in child care. Without careful attention, these movements can cause extreme stress for both children and their families. Having a plan to support the building of new relationships can help ease the stress of transitioning for everyone and help new partnerships develop right from the start.

When meaningful connections are made from the beginning, it creates a foundation to deepen strong relationships over time. Pedagogical leaders can play a crucial role in supporting relationships with families and children by ensuring useful structures are in place.

You may also want to consider:

What is it that we want our families to know about us?

How will we bring visibility to our values and culture?

How might our hallways be a canvas for showing our work?

How do we make cultural and linguistic diversity visible in our programs?

How might families become active contributors to the learning in the program?

How can families get access to information in a way that works best for them?

Where will you keep a history of the child's experiences in the program over time?

How will you discover each family's hopes and dreams for their child?

PEDAGOGICAL LEADERS HELP GROW RELATIONSHIPS BETWEEN THE HUMAN AND NONHUMAN WORLD

Now consider . . .

What is your relationship with the nonhuman world?

What childhood memories do you have about being outside?

What kinds of encounters did you have with plants, water, soil, bugs, or animals?

How do you think those encounters shaped your relationship with the nonhuman world today?

It is impossible to talk about relationships without considering the relationship that we have with the natural world. Just like any other relationship in our lives, the connections we build with the earth can be complex. Whether we consider land to be human property and a provider of natural resources there for the taking or a sacred home, source of knowledge, and giver of life depends largely on our worldview. As human beings, we are part of the natural world and are intrinsically connected to the earth we live on. How we think about that connection has a profound effect on the kinds of relationships we nurture with the world around us.

One of the most critical issues facing children today is the state of the planet we are leaving to them. Early childhood programs are not exempt from the impact of climate change, poor air quality, or the declining health and supply of our water as glaciers recede and deserts expand. Children live in a world that is being dramatically affected by human activity. The relationships they develop with the natural world are formed early, and they learn how to interact and think about the world in large part by observing the adults around them. Pedagogical leaders understand that the relationship educators have with the natural world influences the relationship that children have, and they have a responsibility to rethink the kind of relationships that are being nurtured between children and the nonhuman world. When an educator screams and steps on a bug in the classroom or tells a child to drop a worm because it is dirty, they send powerful messages to children about worthiness, power, and rights. Regardless of whether it is intended or not, the decisions and responses of educators in daily practice have an extraordinary impact on how children learn to perceive their own place in the world.

What could happen if educators were to put greater emphasis on offering experiences that focus on care and connection and how they are living and thinking with the world around them? Claudia and Melissa are co-educators in a preschool classroom. For several weeks they worked closely with pedagogical leader Gabriella to explore ideas around what it means to care for something. On one fall day, near the beginning of their exploration, Claudia and Melissa had planned to take the children on a walk to a reforested area about a mile (2.5 km) from their center.

They were excited for this trip and thought this would be a good way to talk with the children about caring for the environment. They had arranged to start out early so they would have plenty of time to explore. However, as the morning unfolded, everyone's frustrations mounted. It felt as if the children spent most of the time crying and arguing. When it came time to leave, they weren't cooperating, and the walk back took so long that they were all exhausted, grumpy, and late for lunch. Frustrated and disappointed about how the morning unfolded, Claudia declared, "That was the worst walk ever!"

Thankfully, Gabriella had videotaped the experience for them to revisit. As they watched it back, they were surprised at what they saw. The children were far more engaged than they had originally noticed. They witnessed enthusiastic encounters with trees, boulders, and sticks and tender exchanges between children. The educators realized that they had mistook the children's unwillingness to leave this space for crankiness.

Through reflecting on the video with their pedagogical leader, Melissa and Claudia noticed their own disengagement. They could see themselves standing back, taking on the role of distant observer and monitor. They recognized that it was they who had felt pressured for time, and when they tried to rally the children from this beautiful and interesting space, there was resistance.

Revisiting this experience with their pedagogical leader inspired new questions for the group to consider. They asked themselves the following:

> What are we showing that we care about most when we rush children to keep a schedule?
>
> What does it require to build a caring relationship with a place?
>
> What could happen if we as educators brought our own curiosity and care to this space?

These questions led the educators and children to a different kind of encounter the next time they visited the reforested area. Claudia and Melissa began to explore the space alongside the children, wondering, marveling, and imagining together. They began to notice their own roles shifting as they became less concerned about the clock. They noticed their own relationship with the children changing as they moved from offering or imposing experiences to sharing in them. As the educators began to develop their own relationship with the area, conversations with their pedagogical leader evolved. They started to ask questions about the history of the space. Why was it reforested? What was here before? How does understanding the history of a place influence how you care for it?

With Gabriella's guidance, these new questions led Claudia and Melissa to research the area. They learned that this place once had been filled with white oak trees planted by Indigenous people for future generations. While many of the white oaks were gone, there was one in particular that still had a stately presence in the area. In their original walk they had not paid much attention to this tree, but as their relationship with this space started to change, they found themselves deeply drawn to it.

They learned that this tree was more than 675 years old and was a meeting place for asylum seekers who were escaping slavery through the Underground Railroad. Instead of asking how we care for the trees, they began to consider how the trees have cared for the people. This subtle shift in thinking helped them reimagine their original question, "What does it mean to care?" They had unconsciously entered the project with a one-sided notion that it was people who cared for the earth and they had a responsibility to teach children how to do it. However, by nurturing their own curiosity and allowing themselves to build a relationship with a place, it changed both how they saw their role as educators and how they came to think about what it means to care. This magnificent tree had its own story of care. For almost seven centuries it had provided homes, nutrients, and refuge for countless creatures. The idea that caring is not a one-sided act reserved for humans has a powerful impact on how we view our relationship with the land.

Our pedagogical leaders continually share stories like this one throughout the programs in our organizations, inspiring others to take up and sustain this nourishing work. Spreading the values, approaches, and importance of all of these relationships is one of the most critical aspects of the work we do as leaders.

> *"I appreciate the patience and dedication that my pedagogical leader has in keeping us coming back to ideas so that we can consider them more deeply. Over the past year we have been exploring what a classroom curriculum can look like when humans aren't at the center of all of our decisions. It is difficult and challenging work because it is not how we have been used to thinking. It is revealing things to me about myself that I didn't know, and it is bringing a greater awareness to my decision-making."*
>
> *Louisa, educator*

Exploring Your Own Practice: Reflecting on What It Means to Care

The role of the pedagogical leader in this exploration was pivotal in helping educators reconsider the role they have in nurturing healthy, respectful relationships with the natural world. The project inspired them all to ask a new set of questions that has helped develop a different understanding of what it means to care. Use these same questions to engage with educators in conversation and consider:

How does caring for something change us?

What can children teach us about caring?

Do only humans care?

How does knowing the history of a place change our relationship with it?

What does it mean to enter into a relationship with a place?

Is caring a public matter?

Relationships are the glue that holds all other pedagogical principles together. In this chapter we have highlighted just a few ways that you might nurture relationships in your work. As you continue to explore the principles in this book, you will find many other examples of how relationships play a pivotal part in the work of a pedagogical leader. You will see the complexity that exists in growing meaningful relationships and how they can enable you to create a program culture that is built around kindness and curiosity.

RECAPPING THE ROLE OF THE PEDAGOGICAL LEADER IN BUILDING MEANINGFUL RELATIONSHIPS

Pedagogical leaders . . .

- Resist the temptation for short-term quick fixes.
- Hold educators in the same deep regard that they want the educators to hold children.
- Work side by side with educators in their classrooms to really see children.
- Work from a place of curiosity, removing judgment.
- Ask questions rather than providing solutions.
- Help educators to learn from their own experiences and feel successful.
- Provide time, space, and purposeful questions for teams or groups to come together to consider what they want to grow in their classrooms.
- Create a list of shared agreements around what they will need from one another to grow a respectful, safe, and equitable learning environment.
- Engage in deeper dialogue to explore how agreements will look in practice.
- Use agreements to set a foundation to learn more about each other and work together.
- Revisit agreements from time to time to reflect on what is working, what individuals are learning about each other, and how these shared agreements are influencing relationships in the classroom and the program as a whole.
- Understand that positive relationships rely on trust.
- Understand and pay attention to the way they listen to educators.
- Strive to listen from a place of authentic curiosity and empathetic listening.
- Use questions to clarify, probe, and understand viewpoints.
- Support educators to find a way forward without trying to fix or solve the problem for them.

CHAPTER FOUR

Pedagogical Leaders See and Support Competence in Children and Adults

"We like to say that the child is competent, but it is not enough just to declare this. If we really want the child to be competent, we have to change time, space, roles, and rules to permit this competent child to exist."

Carlina Rinaldi, former director of the School of Reggio Emilia

Take a moment to consider . . .

What does competence mean to you?

Where did your ideas about competence come from?

A few years ago, while sitting in her garden, Anne Marie overheard two young boys playing in the yard next to her. They were wielding sticks at each other in what could best be described as a sword fight dance. There was no adult around to stop them as they dodged and ducked each other's imaginary swords, replaying dramatic death scenes over and over.

"I am going to stab you and you fall down." "You are dead now, OK?" "OK, now I will be dead, and you can stab me." Over and over again each of the boys took turns succumbing to the power of the other. When one would fall, the other would help him back up again, often apologizing when they pushed too hard. What struck Anne Marie most as she watched and listened to these two young boys replay this sword fight dance over and over was that this was not a fight at all. Even though they were role-playing death scenes, what she witnessed in their lively exchange was a deep sense of empathy and compassion toward one another. Under the facade of a fight, there was cooperation, agility, resourcefulness, negotiation, reciprocity, and a shared investment in an idea.

Children and adults both display their abilities in a myriad of ways. The kinds of competencies that pedagogical leaders and educators see in others depends on what they are looking for and what they think it means to be competent. Historically, early childhood educators have been trained in child development theory and have been handed down a set of specific developmental milestones against which to measure competence. We have been taught to revere the young child who has a large vocabulary, who can name colors and shapes, or who learns to count, read, or write at an early age. While we would not disagree that these things are important, we also believe that traditional ways of measuring competence are narrow and are rooted in a singular ideology that emphasizes certain skills, knowledge, and abilities as worthy while discounting others.

Thankfully, over the past several years, many North American educators, including ourselves, have been highly influenced by different early learning approaches that have been developing in our own country and around the world. The thinking and practices of teachers from places like Reggio Emilia, Italy; Aotearoa New Zealand; and the Netherlands, as well as thinking with Indigenous worldviews, is helping us expand our ideas about what competence can look like in both children and adults.

In *How Does Learning Happen? Ontario's Pedagogy for the Early Years,* there are clear statements about children, families, and educators being competent and capable (Ontario Public Service 2014). Similar declarations can be found in many other early learning curriculums across Canada and the United States. Yet we know that competence is a social construct, and different communities and cultures have different ideas about it. In order for us to see competence in others, we must explore where our ideas about competence come from. We must be willing to ask different kinds of questions:

What do I think it means to be competent?

What stories about competence did I grow up with?

Who decides what it means to be competent?

Is the competent child or adult the one who simply follows directions or does what they are told?

Do I need to be able to see and name competence in another for it to exist?

How do I see competence in others who are different from me?

If we are to expand our ideas about competence, we must be willing to look beyond child development theory alone and consider multiple ways to see and listen. You may be familiar with the story of the animal school where each student was measured against the same criteria. The fish failed miserably in flying class, the eagle flunked the tunnel-digging course, and so on. It is a story that emphasizes the problem with a standardized education system that measures children against each other, advantages some over others, and doesn't acknowledge or nurture the diverse gifts that individuals have. It is a familiar system that leaves us believing that some of us are "smart" and some of us aren't.

As we said, we are not suggesting that children shouldn't learn to read and write or recognize numbers. Of course, these are skills we all find useful in managing our way through society. What we are interested in doing is disrupting the idea that those are the *only* competencies worth noting and nurturing.

What could happen if the purpose of early education was to help children (and adults) uncover their own gifts and learn how to give them back to the world? The potential of human beings is enormous and varied, but unless opportunities exist to grow those potentials, they can easily be lost. When it comes to seeing and supporting competence in others, there are several things that a pedagogical leader can do.

Pedagogical leaders . . .

- Focus on strengths.
- Remove judgment and appraisal and focus on learning.
- Support educators to see children's competence.
- Nurture risk competence in children and adults.

PEDAGOGICAL LEADERS FOCUS ON STRENGTHS

Now consider . . .

What strengths do you bring to your work?

What kinds of things do you look forward to doing every day?

In our experience, we often find that it is easier for people to list their areas of weakness than it is to talk about their strengths. Perhaps it is because many of us were taught to be humble, and talking about what we are good at can seem boastful. Maybe it is because most of us were raised in an education system where the only gifts that were acknowledged were those that fell into a very particular category and the grade you received determined how smart you were. Perhaps, in part, it is because we live in a world where instead of embracing the beautiful learning journey that we are all on, we get a constant nagging feeling that we are not ready. We often hear how infant educators feel pressured to get babies ready to move into the toddler room. Likewise, toddler educators often feel like they need to get children ready for preschool. And so it goes, the pressure on educators to prepare children for what is to come next continues throughout our lives until the only thing we have left to prepare for is our own funeral. We do wonder if this mindset of needing to constantly get ready for a life that has been prescribed by others has left generations of people with the feeling that they are not good enough—especially those whose natural-born gifts might be a little different. What if instead of training the masses toward the same end, we could find a way to build on individual strengths?

> *"By looking at others from a place of strength, I have learned that there are so many different ways of thinking and being in this world. Focusing on what people can do and not what they can't do actually helps support my own learning and growth. As a pedagogical leader it takes the pressure off me feeling like I have to know everything. When I can recognize their individual strengths, it widens my perspective and in turn grows my practice. We really are better together."*
>
> ~ *Angela, pedagogical leader*

Working from strengths means valuing the skills, knowledge, passions, and potential of an individual. It doesn't mean ignoring challenges or spinning weaknesses into perceived strengths. Whether it be their own strengths or those of the educators they are working with, it is important that pedagogical leaders believe that strengths exist and learn to see how strength shows up differently in different people.

Human beings are unlimited and varied in their potential, and often educators bring with them skills, talents, and deep interests that at first glance might not seem relevant yet could very well be extraordinarily valuable to their work. Some may not be aware of the strengths they have and need assistance in seeing them. Regardless, believing that everyone has something valuable to offer is the first step in creating a space where people can bring their best selves. Listen to how pedagogical leader Maria helped an educator bring out her gifts through a center project.

Maria was a new pedagogical leader at a large child care center. This was the first time that this center had anyone in this role, and there was much excitement and anticipation around what Maria would bring to their work. One of the first things that she was tasked with was purchasing some much-needed toys, materials, and equipment for the three preschool classrooms. Rather than deciding on her own about how to spend the money, Maria thought it was important for the educators to be involved in the decision-making. She arranged a series of meetings and visits with the six preschool educators involved. She wanted them to dream about what they might like for their classrooms and why. She asked them to take some time to write down their thoughts.

She encouraged the educators to do an inventory of the toys and materials that they already had and offered them some targeted questions to begin with.

> What are the things the children seem to find the most pleasure playing with in your classroom?
>
> What are the things that you find pleasure in?
>
> What items need to be repaired or replaced?
>
> What items need to be discarded or given away and why?
>
> What new toys, materials, or equipment would you like to add and why?

Together they revisited their center vision and talked about what they wanted for the children and themselves. As they continued to spend time together and imagine new possibilities for their classrooms, Maria noticed that Shelly had disengaged from the conversations. Maria learned that Shelly had worked in the center for more than thirty years. When Maria invited her to share her thoughts, Shelly just said that she was good with whatever the others decided. Maria didn't feel right about forcing Shelly into the conversations, yet she felt strongly about wanting her to feel like a part of the planning and decision-making. Through conversations and classroom visits, Maria felt like she was getting to know five of the educators quite well, but Shelly remained a mystery. She decided that if she really wanted to get to know Shelly, she would have to engage her differently. So she started to talk to her about life outside of the center. Maria learned that Shelly was a grandmother, and one of her favorite things to do was to spend time in her garden. She discovered that Shelly was the one who had brought all the plants into the center, and it was she who lovingly tended them. Maria learned that Shelly was part of the local horticulture club and had won awards and hosted multiple garden tours. Maria could see clearly that when Shelly talked about gardening, she lit up. As they continued their conversations, Maria suggested that perhaps they could expand the classroom transformation to include part of the children's playground. Shelly's expertise could be such a gift in helping them to reimagine their outdoor spaces. What resulted was more than any of them could have imagined. Not only did Shelly bring a renewed energy to her work and begin to see that she had something important to contribute, the invitation to bring her passion transformed the entire center's relationship with their outdoor spaces. Her work and enthusiasm resulted in the formation of a new playground committee. What started out as a small initiative to add some plants to the preschool playground ended up morphing into a yearlong project where the entire center reimagined its relationships with its outdoor spaces and the creatures that shared them. Shelly's younger colleagues were amazed at what she knew and started to see her as a mentor. Shelly, who had never taken to documentation, started to write daily about her and the children's experiences in the garden.

By taking a strengths-based approach, Maria helped Shelly to see that she had something very important to offer and helped her find a way into writing more about her work, something that had challenged her in the past. Maria was able to create a situation where the educators could see strengths in each other and value the diverse contributions that each of them could make. Ultimately, through this experience Maria was able to assist the educators to transform both their spaces and how they saw each other in their work. Shelly, who had planned on an early retirement, ended up staying at the center for another five years.

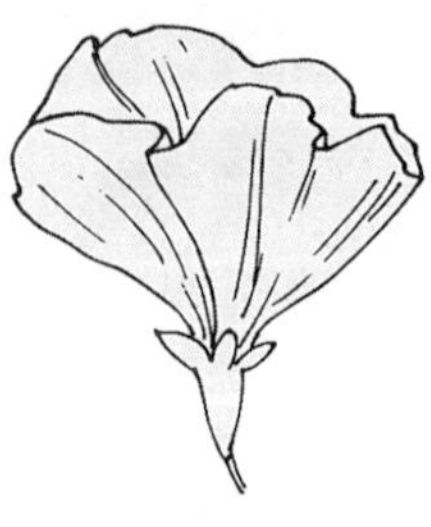

Pause and Reflect

What do you know about the people you work with?

What passions do they have?

How do they enjoy spending their time when they are not at work?

When pedagogical leaders create opportunities for educators to bring their own gifts and talents to their work, it can result in benefits that reach far beyond just one individual. It can nurture a learning community where difference is welcome and respected. It can evoke feelings of worthiness, create a sense of belonging, and provide pathways to improve skills in different areas. Working from strengths means creating a culture where everyone is seen as having something important to offer.

> *"Demonstrating respect for my colleagues and focusing on their strengths allows me to seek to understand when we find ourselves at a difference of opinion. I am able to set emotion aside from the equation and view the situation from their perspective."*
>
> ~ *Jen, educator*

Just as pedagogical leaders can hold educators up by focusing on strengths, so too can educators hold up children. Listen to what happens as Angela uses a strengths-based approach to help two boys in her classroom work through a problem.

Angela's lively group of preschool children had spent the morning working together to create a large intricate pathway out of blocks and wooden stumps. The structure they created turned into a backdrop for a popular game the children excitedly referred to as Hot Lava. The goal seemed to be to move across the pathway without stepping on the floor (aka the hot lava). The children were highly invested in this game and were quite adept at moving through the pathway without falling. At one point, however, Jack and Hayden came face-to-face and found themselves at an impasse. Neither of the boys wanted to step on the ground to let the other pass. When it became clear that neither was willing to move, Jack, who was quite a bit bigger and used to using his size to his advantage, puffed up his body and grabbed Hayden by the shoulders as if to physically move him. Angela noticed what had been happening and approached the two children.

Pause and Reflect

What might your first response be to a situation like this and why?

How might you approach this from a strengths-based perspective?

Instead of stopping the game or trying to solve the problem for them, Angela acknowledged the boys' dilemma. She said, "I can see that you both want to pass by each other." Jack then responded, "Hayden is in my way. He needs to move." Angela reminded the children of their shared commitment to the game and began to describe what she saw happening prior to the boys' impasse. "I was watching you both work so hard with the other children to build this magnificent structure. You spent so long together making it, and you seem to be having so much fun. Now you have a problem. How do you think we can figure this out?" Jack, seeming a bit agitated, continued to insist that Hayden move out of his way. Hayden, who tended to be the one to give in situations like this, quietly stepped out of the way. Rather than simply letting the children go about their play, Angela made a point of saying to both boys, "Thank you, Hayden. That was a very kind thing you just did for Jack. You both worked so hard to build this game, and you are being a good friend to let Jack through." Hayden gave a shy smile, and both boys carried on leaping across the block pathway. A short time later, they found themselves at the same impasse. This time, however, Angela noticed that Jack got out of the way for Hayden. She made a point of saying, "Oh Jack, now you are being a good friend to Hayden." This lovely exchange could have ended right there with both boys feeling pleased about themselves. However, Angela believed that this was an important opportunity to highlight the children's kindness toward each other and wanted to find a way to bring attention to what she saw. At circle time the next morning, she offered the children photos of the great construction they had created together the day before and invited the children to talk about their experience. Then she reminded Jack and Hayden about their impasse and invited the boys to share with the other children what had happened. Jack enthusiastically retold the story, sharing how he and Hayden had worked through their problem by being good friends and by moving out of the way for each other. This declaration seemed to be particularly important for Jack. As he recalled the way he worked through this problem with Hayden, Jack inspired a larger discussion among all the children about what being a good friend can look like.

Angela assisted the children by helping them be their best selves in that moment. She intentionally pointed out the strengths that each of them showed in the situation, and then she created a space for them to remember what they had done and share it with others. This intentional response resulted in an important classroom conversation about kindness and friendship and enabled Jack to see and articulate his own competence and that of his friend Hayden.

Both of these stories demonstrate how focusing on what a person can do, rather than what they can't or aren't doing, can help people see that they have something valuable to offer. It creates a space for an individual to continually refine their gifts, and in doing so it inspires learning along the way. Focusing on people's strengths requires that pedagogical leaders embrace the vast and diverse ways that people live in the world. It reinforces the idea that everyone has something unique and relevant to offer and disrupts the notion that everyone learns the same way and must know how to do the same things. Instead, it sets a stage where people can use their own unique abilities to strengthen the larger community.

Exploring Pedagogical Practice: Uncovering Your Own Strengths

Consider using the following questions to reflect on your own gifts. Invite others to complete the questions as well, and share answers so that you can learn more about the gifts and strengths that others bring to your learning community.

www.redleafpress.org/crp/d-7.pdf

Uncovering Your Strengths

What do you enjoy doing so much that you lose track of time?

What is important to you about life?

What do others say you are good at?
(mentors, colleagues, family members, friends)

Describe three or four situations where you have felt most successful.

Seeing Strengths in Children

Just as we can use questions to uncover our own strengths, educators can take up this same practice with the children in their care.

Child's name	What words would you use to describe this child's strengths, skills, and interests?	What opportunities and experiences do you currently offer in the classroom for this child to grow their strengths?	What new opportunities might you offer?

www.redleafpress.org/crp/d-8.pdf

What stood out to you when you were going through the exercise? Was it an easier task with some children over others? What does it have you thinking about in terms of your environment and relationships with each child?

"Focusing on strengths has been a pivotal leadership practice for me, and in embracing this approach to life and leadership, it lit a fire for curiosity, deepening my desire to better understand humans through listening, questioning, and empathy. The relationship that I have with educators and colleagues is deeper and more engaged. I see people through a completely new light; we all have strengths, and we can all be successful when someone is willing to work with us within those strengths."

Julie, pedagogical leader

When pedagogical leaders hold the belief that each person, big or small, has unique qualities and gifts, they can help provide a space where those gifts can be nurtured and shared with others. Believing that each person has something valuable to offer helps to create an environment where people feel like they matter. It reinforces the idea that people can and do live differently in the world and that each person is worthy and relevant. Acknowledging that no one person is great at everything but that everyone has something to offer can help create a learning environment where both educators and pedagogical leaders are open to learning from each other.

Working from strengths can help create a confidence and willingness in people to name the things they are good at and the things they want to learn more about. It creates feelings of competence that lead to a growth mindset, where individuals learn to believe in their own ability to learn new things.

To see the strength that exists in others, we must be able to acknowledge and appreciate what makes people different and create a space where everyone is included and valued. Gender, race, language, ethnicity, sexual orientation, religion, ability, and age are all things that help to make up who we are. Yet we know that systemic barriers, stereotyping, and bias often make it very difficult for people to share themselves and their gifts.

How do you get to know people who are different from you?

What can you do to learn more about the systemic barriers that exist in your organization?

PEDAGOGICAL LEADERS REMOVE JUDGMENT AND APPRAISAL AND FOCUS ON LEARNING

Now consider . . .

Have you ever been misunderstood?

What kinds of questions help you understand others' thinking and behavior?

When was the last time you made an assumption or a judgment about another person, only to find out later you were wrong? Did you base your assumption on a first impression or on the person's behavior or appearance? Did the person remind you of a past experience or someone you once knew? Has anyone made an assumption about you? Have you ever felt misunderstood? As human beings who are intrinsically connected to each other, the reality is that there is far more that we don't know about each other than we do. Yet still we make assumptions about each other all the time.

Our assumptions are often based on our own beliefs, biases, experiences, and relationships. They often lead us to judgment and can stop us from gaining a deeper understanding of each other. One of the greatest problems with assumptions and judgments is that they can quickly turn into a single story that we convince ourselves is true. It is important that pedagogical leaders notice when they start to make assumptions and judgments. When they notice this happening, they need to focus their energy on learning and understanding. Rather than rushing to judgment, rush to curiosity. It may sound easy: just stop judging and remain curious. The truth is that it isn't easy, and it takes a great deal of personal reflection and mindfulness practice. In her book *Change Your Questions, Change Your Life,* author Marilee Adams (2016) talks about the learner/judger mindset and offers us the notion that we can choose. We can choose to stay in a judger mindset or take a new path to the learner mindset. It takes a practice of pausing and taking notice of when we are judging. It requires that we consider what triggers us to judge and to make a conscious decision to stay curious and be open to learning.

"Every child has a story to tell, and within that story is the secret to reaching her or him as a learner. Children's stories are windows into their uniqueness and clues on how to connect the child and the curriculum."

Herb Kohl, educator and writer

This quote holds true of our work with educators. What if as pedagogical leaders we considered that each educator has a story to tell and that within that story is the secret to reaching them as a learner? How might we go about trying to understand that story? What might happen if we chose to stay curious about why people do what they do? Why do they make the decisions they do? Too often we make up stories based on our own understandings and assumptions. Has that ever happened to you? If we want educators to be curious about children's thinking, we also have to be curious about educators' thinking. Listen to the story of a program leader who is encouraged to stay curious and how this curiosity leads to greater learning for both the educator and the pedagogical leader.

As a leader in a large child care program for nearly ten years, Carmen felt well grounded in her practice. She had strong relationships with the educators, children, and families. The team was well established, and many of them had been at the program since it had opened nearly twenty-five years ago. Over the last several years, the program had begun to shift from a theme-based curriculum to a more emergent approach. The shift was a huge learning curve for many. As a leader, Carmen wanted the team to have all the resources they needed to be successful with the change. She purchased books, sought out professional learning opportunities, and supported changes to the classroom environments.

She developed schedules that offered teams a bit of time each week to document and plan for their classrooms. As part of the curriculum, educators were now required to document children's learning. They started writing daily journals for children, taking photos, and writing stories of children's learning and posting them on their walls. It wasn't easy, but most of the educators were finding their way. Over the course of just a few years, there was a shift in practice. Documenting was becoming a part of educator practice, and the walls started to fill with images and stories from the classrooms. It had become an expectation for educators to document. The transition had been easier for some educators than others.

Carmen had noticed that Janice, one of the infant educators, hadn't been posting any documentation. The other team members had also come and spoken to Carmen on several occasions, frustrated that they were doing all the documenting in the classroom. Wanting to offer support, Carmen provided additional time to Janice and offered her several opportunities for professional learning as well. Her hope was to give Janice all the support she needed to be successful—but it just wasn't working. Janice was still not taking up the practice of documenting. Carmen was becoming more and more frustrated and felt as though Janice was just avoiding the work and being lazy. Finally, after many conversations, goal setting, and professional learning opportunities, Carmen was at her wits' end. She carefully crafted a letter for Janice that stated that she was not meeting the requirements of her role and that further noncompliance would result in her dismissal. It wasn't an easy letter to write: Janice was a long-term employee and she had lovely relationships with the children and families, but part of her role was to document children's learning. Carmen felt she had no other choice because if she didn't make it a requirement for everyone, she would be setting a precedent. As part of a larger organization, Carmen contacted her program director, Jenna, to let her know of the plan to present the letter to Janice later that day.

Pause and Reflect

What might you do in this situation, and why?

What supports do you have to think through these kinds of challenging situations?

Jenna asked Carmen to hold onto the letter until they could meet later that day. When she arrived, Jenna read the letter that Carmen had drafted and asked Carmen if she felt that the letter would support Janice in being successful. Throwing her hands up in frustration, Carmen said she didn't know what else to do. She had put in place time for additional planning and offered numerous resources and professional learning opportunities, and yet still Janice refused to document. Jenna, curious, asked Carmen, "Why do you think she isn't documenting?" "I don't think she really cares. She hates change and resists any changes," Carmen replied. "Have you ever asked her why she refuses to document?" Jenna inquired. "No, not really, but it seems clear that she doesn't want to do the work," Carmen responded. Curious, Jenna wondered what might happen if instead of handing Janice the letter, they met with her and asked her why she wasn't doing the work required.

Later that afternoon, Carmen met with Janice, and the conversation brought to light much that Carmen didn't know. When asked why she continued to refuse to document, Janice simply stated that she thought it was a waste of time and not at all useful. Surprised by the response, Carmen delved a bit deeper, asking what she meant by "waste of time" and "not useful." Janice shared that she felt that documenting was very clinical and boring. It dawned on Carmen that perhaps Janice's refusal to document might be more about her fear of getting it wrong or being too clinical than with laziness. Perhaps Janice's resistance was masking her fear. Perhaps Carmen's assumptions about why Janice wasn't doing the work were getting in the way of learning what supports Janice actually needed.

Carmen then asked Janice to share a story of a moment in the classroom that touched her. She thought for a bit, and then her face lit up. She shared a story of an interaction she had watched between two infants on their morning walk. She talked about how they seemed to have a language of their own, and she loved watching how they listened and responded to each other without words. It was a beautiful story. Carmen suggested that she document and share that story. Janice was hesitant at first, but as she talked it through more with Carmen, she started to feel more reassured that these kinds of everyday moments were important and worthy of sharing. Carmen encouraged Janice to write about the moments with children that delighted her and captured her attention, rather than trying to qualify everything against a developmental checklist. As Janice wrote more, her classroom stories provided a focus for conversation and reflection. In a short time, her confidence about her own work grew. She began to share her writing with her team. Together they reflected on their writings to notice the different ways that children were learning about each other and the world around them. Families looked forward to hearing about these moments and often shared their appreciation. The team grew stronger, and Janice could see the power of documentation.

When pedagogical leaders stay curious, it can help keep them from going down a judgment path. They can begin to ask questions that can help them better understand the thinking that drives people to do what they do and build the kind of trust where learning can happen.

"It is so easy to go to a judgmental place when something happens that feels outside our own ideas or expectations of those around us. Engaging through questions has opened up space to be truly curious and value another perspective, helping me to better understand their worldview. Even if we don't agree, understanding people's motivations helps us to humanize them and relate to them in a more respective way."

Hanah, pedagogical leader

Exploring Your Own Practice: Moving from Judgment to Curiosity

When you take a path to learning, your questions are open-minded and authentically curious. They invite creative thinking, and they can lead to new understandings, discoveries, and solutions. The next time you find yourself making assumptions or judgments, consider how these questions can take you on a path to curiosity and learning.

What do I think is really happening here?

What else might be happening here?

How might the environment affect what is happening?

How has our culture lent itself to what is happening?

What is my theory about these facts?

What am I responsible for in this situation?

Is my thinking serving others or myself?

What is the story I am making up about this person/situation?

Am I seeing this person's strengths or focusing on their weaknesses?

What are my choices?

What can I learn?

What is the other person feeling, needing, wanting?

Notice how these questions can also support educators in being curious about children's thinking. When we can meet up with the minds of others rather than their behavior, we can focus on learning and in turn build a strong culture where relationships are central to our practice.

PEDAGOGICAL LEADERS SUPPORT EDUCATORS TO SEE CHILDREN'S COMPETENCE

Now consider . . .

What words come to mind for you when you think of the competencies of children? Of educators?

How do you help educators see the competencies of children?

Progressive pedagogical and curriculum frameworks all around the world invite educators to take up the view of the child as capable, competent, and full of wonder and curiosity. The more we learn about how learning happens, early brain development, and the true capacity of young children, the more our practice needs to align to this competent viewpoint.

When we authors started out in the early learning field more than thirty years ago, our work in the classroom revolved around themes, or topics that we decided as educators. The themes often centered around seasons, animals, the solar system, dinosaurs, and so on. As educators, we researched the facts, earnestly gathered materials to decorate our walls and dramatic centers, created art activities, and learned songs and fingerplays connected to the themes. We did a great deal of planning for our circles and tabletop activities all in an effort to teach children the facts about the theme. We loved our work and took great pride in our practice. It was what we knew. In retrospect, this practice, although well intentioned, did not meet up with the brilliance of children. We were taught to see children as if they needed to be filled with knowledge, rather than seeing them as natural researchers.

In the first three years of life, children learn to talk and walk. They begin to master their body and develop important relationships. Children are brilliant researchers who gather information, make predictions, test theories, and make discoveries. In fact, we would suggest that babies and young children are the most competent researchers and learners on earth. They are quite literally built to figure out how the world around them works.

A pedagogical leader can support educators as they take up observing and researching these brilliant humans to gain a deeper understanding of what they already know and are learning about. When pedagogical leaders work together with educators to observe competence, it changes them. What we have learned is that once you see children's competence, you can no longer not see it.

In their book *From Teaching to Thinking,* Ann Pelo and Margie Carter invite us to reimagine our practice. They challenge us to rethink our role as leaders and emphasize the value of engaging in questions rather than offering or looking for answers. We agree and encourage educators to reflect with others, to see themselves as researchers and thinkers. "Neither curriculum books brimming with activities nor detailed assessment checklists cultivate the practice of research. We don't need scripts or lesson plans, but protocols for disciplined and reflective study—protocols for inquiry—research protocols" (2018, 164).

Pause and Reflect

How has your practice evolved over time?

How does your knowledge of children's competence influence your practice?

"One specific example for me was the day we sat in the boardroom and my pedagogical leader addressed our frustrations and concerns about a specific child in our preschool room. We made a list on the whiteboard of the good, strong, positive things about this child, reminding us of what we had lost track of in our complicated feelings. We also addressed the specifics of what we were really concerned about, and then she helped us see each of them with either a work-in-progress 'solution' or a different way to look at things. This showed me a way to identify what works for an individual child, that it is not always what works for the group, and that it is OK to build a program around that."

Stacy, educator

It is important that pedagogical leaders take time to explore children's competence alongside educators. Learning about what children know and understand about the world around them is a practice that deserves continuous attention.

We have seen a palpable shift in educators' practice when they focus on what children know and understand rather than what they see as disruptive behaviors and problems. The kinds of things that pedagogical leaders and educators focus their attention on in the classroom matter, and these focuses shape how they come to think about themselves and others as well as the importance of their work. If you want to grow kindness in your classroom, then give kindness your attention and make an intentional decision to look for it, name it, and bring visibility to it. Consider how Judy, a pedagogical leader in a toddler program, helped educators consider a question that helped them focus on and study children's competence.

The toddler room is often a busy spot in the morning as children are arriving and settling in to their day. On this particular morning there was a sense of joyful calm in the room, as the children were scattered throughout, engaged in a variety of experiences. Evie, a twenty-one-month-old, arrived later than usual that morning and had a hard time separating from her mom. Educator Wendy greeted Evie and her mom, and with some tears Evie went into Wendy's arms. She stayed with Wendy for a few minutes but then wanted to get down. She went off to the quiet area, selected a book, and sat down. A few minutes later, another child arrived. Evie watched carefully and tears started to well up in her eyes, and she started to quietly cry again for her mom. Lucas, another one of the toddlers, noticed. He went over to the baskets in the room that held the children's blankets, soothers, and other comfort items. He carefully selected Evie's blanket and soother and took it to her in the quiet area. He sat beside her and cocked his head ever so slightly to give her a kiss on the cheek. The educators in the room noticed and smiled at each other across the room. They loved witnessing these sweet moments.

Later that day in the staff room, Wendy was sharing the story with the team in the preschool room. They all shared their awe at this beautiful moment and started telling stories from their own classrooms where they had noticed children being kind to one another. Wendy mentioned that she hadn't really noticed this before in the toddler room but wished it happened more. Judy, the pedagogical leader, wondered if it wasn't happening or if they just weren't noticing it. Judy was aware of how busy a toddler room could be and wondered if the image often portrayed of toddlers as "terrible twos" might be affecting how the educators were seeing the children. As the pedagogical leader, Judy wanted to help the toddler team see that these moments were not random but happened all the time. In their next team meeting, Judy brought up the story again and asked the team to consider the words that came to mind when they reflected on it. The words *kind, empathy, caring, friend, thoughtful, observant,* and *connection* came up, among others.

Judy then asked which of those words or ideas they were curious to learn more about. The word *friend* sparked a lively conversation.

Using the word *friend* as a beginning point, Judy offered the team a large piece of flip chart paper and wrote and circled the word in the middle of the page. Handing each educator a stack of sticky notes, she asked them to brainstorm words that came to mind when they thought of the word *friend*. It wasn't long before the paper was covered with dozens of words that connected. Together they began to group the notes and words into different categories. They came up with many ways children show friendship to one another, the emotions that kindness and friendship evoke, and different acts of friendship. The process of sorting through words and ideas together generated conversations that helped them reflect on their classroom and wonder what more might be happening.

Judy drew on their conversations and words and helped them tease out a question that they were curious to use as a focus for their observation and study in the classroom. It took some time, but after much discussion they landed on the following question: What strategies do toddlers use to build connections with one another?

To support the team, Judy asked more questions to explore the topic they selected to be sure that they were truly curious about it and that it would shed light on children's competencies.

Is the question of interest to the whole team and potentially to others? Is this a question that the team is eager to explore together?

Is it an idea we want to shed light on and something we are trying to grow?

Does the question help us see children's competencies?

Will we be able to observe the question in children's play?

Will we be able to collect notes, photos, and videos connected to the question?

The educators were excited at the prospect of this work and talked about ways they share their learning together. They also shared a desire to bring their discoveries to families and others in the program. Seeing this excitement, Judy wanted to pause the team to make some intentional decisions about how they would collect and share their observations. Using these questions, the team made a plan for moving forward.

What resources will you need to compile your observations?

What research could be taken up to learn more about this idea?

What methods will you use to collect your observations?

How will we bring visibility to your process? Where could this research question live in the classroom?

What systems might be useful for organizing and storing your work?

How will we ensure time to reflect on and study your data with others?

How will we engage families in the research question or process?

The questions helped the group think about a way forward, understanding that these questions would be revisited over time. Over the next several weeks the educators would take notes and photos and together observe the strategies children were using to build connections. Rest time became a time to debrief what they were noticing, and team meetings had a focus on studying the videos, photos, and notes they gathered throughout the day. The list of strategies they noticed was long, and it included actions they hadn't noticed before. They enjoyed watching children use humor, catching others' attention using subtle ways like eye contact and gentle physical contact, and enticing friends with materials and ideas. The conversations at their team meetings were shifting, and they spent their time talking about the brilliance of these very young people. Their image of toddlers was evolving, and the stories they shared with families showed these children's competence in building relationships.

When the educators reflected on what they had learned, they noticed that families seemed more engaged and excited to hear the daily stories. Educators reflected on their own roles and saw themselves watching longer and stepping in less. They felt their observations really challenged their former misconceptions of toddlers. Their curiosity was contagious, and as they reflected on their observations, new questions were sparked: How do children use humor to grow relationships? What do children already know about getting along together? What materials in the classroom bring children together?

Choosing a lens or question to have as a focus can offer educators a way of seeing, growing, and sharing children's competence. When pedagogical leaders help educators take up this lens, it can offer a way for teams to focus on children's strengths and design both the physical and social and emotional environment in response to what they see. In the words of an educator who took up this practice:

"Through researching with toddlers, I have grown and learned so much. It is one of the most rewarding experiences, seeing the children also grow and learn. Researching has opened my mind and encouraged me to think deeper about what children are doing and why they are doing it. I have grown as an educator by researching and reflecting with my team. I am able to explore with the children and support their ideas. I truly believe that researching with children has given my profession as an educator a much stronger purpose."

~ Vicky, pedagogical leader

Begin with Curiosity

Coming up with an interesting question is one way to build curiosity around what children know and what they can do, to observe children's competence in the classroom.

Talk with educator teams to learn more about what they are paying attention to in the children's play. What recurring themes do they notice? What are they learning about children's relationships with each other and the world around them? These observations can act as a guide to what you want to learn more about.

Create a Word Cloud

Consider a word that connects with the big idea educators are noticing and want to learn more about.

Using flip chart paper and sticky notes, the team considers as many words as possible that connect to the big idea. Once the group feels it has exhausted the words connected to the big idea, consider using an internet search, a thesaurus, or a dictionary to expand thinking.

Sort the notes into three or four categories that make sense to the team. Once you have had a chance to think through these subgroups, together decide which area you want to focus your research on.

Tease Out a Question

Together choose one or two questions the group is curious about to study in the classroom. The question should connect to competencies of children and be something that you want to see more and grow in the classroom.

Questions to help you evaluate your questions:

- Is the question one that is of interest to the whole team and potentially to others? Is this a question that the team is eager to explore together?
- Is it an idea you want to shed light on and something you are trying to grow?
- Does the question explore seeing children's competencies?
- Is the question one that you will be able to see every day?
- Will you be able to collect notes, photos, and videos connected to the question?

Consider How You Will Organize and Collect Observations.

- What resources will you need to compile your observations?
- What research could be taken up to learn more about this idea?
- What methods will you use to collect your observations?
- How will we bring visibility to your process? Where could this research question live in the classroom?
- What systems might be useful for organizing and storing your work?
- How will we ensure time to reflect on and study your data with others?
- How will we engage families in the research question or process?

Reflect on Your Observations

Studying your data is a critical part of the process and allows you to choose a response or move back in to observe more. There are many protocols that you may find useful to guide you through the reflective process. Protocols such as the Thinking Lens® offer thoughtful questions and processes to engage educators in dialogue. This is also a good time to reevaluate your question and see what new curiosities may be evolving.

Exploring Pedagogical Practice: Creating a Lens to See Competence

The following structure was used by the pedagogical leader in the previous story and can be used as a guide for pedagogical leaders to develop questions as a lens for observing.

PEDAGOGICAL LEADERS NURTURE RISK COMPETENCE IN CHILDREN AND ADULTS

Now consider . . .

How would you describe your relationship to risk?

What kinds of risks are you willing to take?

What kinds of risks are you averse to?

As adults, we all have different comfort levels with taking risks. We are influenced by our past experience, our environment, and our personality, as well as our beliefs around risks and risk-taking. Pedagogical leaders work with educators who have varied feelings around the subject, ranging from those who are completely risk averse to those who are eager risk-takers. The feelings and ideas that educators have personally about taking risks often infiltrate how they approach risk-taking with children. While no one would dispute that it is of paramount importance to keep children safe, it is crucial that we question what it means to be safe while also taking risks.

Our brains are wired for risk because we live in a world where risks are a daily reality. Whether taking our first steps, crossing a street, applying for a new job, falling in love, sharing an opinion, speaking up against an injustice, or simply trying something new, we are all faced with a multitude of risks every day. Not only is it impossible not to take risks, but to resist them means to resist living and growing and goes against the very nature of what makes us human.

Every early childhood educator knows that to try to stop a toddler from climbing is futile. There are no barriers that can stop the persistent drive they have to push their body quite literally to new heights. We see the same thing on playgrounds all across the county where young children who have mastered going down the slide are then driven to climb up it. This is not defiant behavior but a masterful brain at work, continuously driving the body to challenge itself. That insistent and familiar "me do" attitude that drives children to want to try things for themselves is what pushes them to take not just physical risks but also social, emotional, and intellectual risks. Early childhood educators make multiple decisions every day that can either stop children from taking risks or help them learn to recognize and navigate risks safely. Understanding the difference between the risks that are challenging and those that are dangerous is the key to keeping children safe. Educators can play an important role in helping young children develop risk competence when they themselves feel like competent risk-takers.

Consider a situation that Andrea, a preschool educator, faced when challenged by a child's risk-taking endeavors. The center where she works has a large common play area, overlooked by the main floor of the building. It is a bright, engaging space with large windows that span over two stories, and children often delight in shouting back and forth from the levels as they see each other at play. To get to the lower level, the children travel down a long four-sided ramp that starts on the main floor and winds its way around the perimeter walls to the lower level, where it opens up to a large space. The ramp itself has a guard rail that allows the children to see and experience the vast open space as they move up and down to different floors. The ramp was constructed to provide a safe, protected, and interesting way to travel from one floor to the next, but for young adventurous children it is often a provocation to challenge their bodies. On this particular day, rather than traveling up the intended part of the ramp, four-year-old Marcella shinnied her body on the outside of the rail until she was up so high off the ground that Andrea could not reach her. Rather than telling her to get down, Andrea asked Marcella to pause and look around. It was at that point that Marcella herself seemed to realize how high up she was. Andrea pointed out that she was out of reach and asked her if she felt safe. Marcella looked around and said, "I think I am too high up." Andrea responded by saying, "I was thinking the same thing." At that point, the child carefully started her descent. This was not always how Andrea would have responded to children's risk-taking. It was only a couple of years prior that she saw herself as the classroom police, constantly monitoring and saying no to children more than she said yes. However, with the help of some strong pedagogical leadership, along with her own openness and desire to grow as an educator, she transformed how she thought about risk-taking and learned how to say yes to children's ideas. Listen to how Andrea described how she used to feel about children's risk-taking in her classroom.

While I have always had strong relationships with the children in my classroom, there were many times during the day when the stress levels of both the children and myself were high. Children would have an idea such as standing on furniture to reach higher. I would stop them because I perceived this to be dangerous. They would react by either getting upset or continuing to try and achieve their goal when I wasn't looking. This power struggle made me feel like I was spending my day policing, and I lost the joy in my work. As I began to reflect more on my own practice, I discovered that I was saying no to children's ideas without really pausing to consider the reason why. I recognized that there was a connection between the stress levels in the room and me saying no, and I began to wonder how I might relieve this tension.

Pause and Reflect

Do you ever feel like you say no more than you say yes?

What are the kinds of activities you notice yourself stopping and why?

Andrea's deep desire to have a different experience for both the children and herself opened the door for her to learn more about the impact of her own response to children's risk-taking in the classroom. While Andrea had always been a close observer of children, she hadn't always observed herself. Together with her pedagogical leader, she designed a plan where she would video herself with the children at different times of the day. She set aside time to journal daily about her own emotional and physical responses to children's risk-taking, and she met weekly with her pedagogical leader to discuss what she was noticing. These weekly discussions provided an opportunity to uncover many underlying ideas and reconsider the importance and value of risk-taking. In the past Andrea had mostly thought of the physical aspects,

but she now started to notice just how many different ways that children take risks throughout the day. For example, she realized that children were risking rejection every time they shared their ideas with each other or simply asked if they could play.

Realizing the different ways that children take risks throughout the day helped Andrea understand more about how imperative risk-taking is for growth. It also helped her to realize that rather than stopping children from taking risks, her role was to help children become competent risk-takers. She began to talk openly with children about what it means to take a risk. They talked about the difference between something that is challenging and something that is dangerous, and she helped them notice their surroundings. She brought attention to when they were being brave by sharing a different idea or trying something new and encouraged the children to support each other. Rather than stopping them from taking risks, she started to create intentional spaces for children to challenge themselves and each other in different ways.

Just as children need space to take risks, so too do adults. Reflecting on her practice was in itself a risk for Andrea. It required a kind of vulnerability that enabled her to share her work, question herself openly, and risk criticism from others. Having guidance and support from a pedagogical leader helped Andrea feel safe in her own risk-taking and in turn helped her to support the children.

"As a pedagogical leader I have really come to understand how important discourse is in my learning. When I allow myself to lean into experiences that make me feel uncomfortable, I find these are some of the powerful learning experiences I have. This courage has shaped so much of who I am as a leader."

Clare, pedagogical leader

There has been much written lately on the benefits of risk-taking for young children. While we agree that risk-taking is important for learning, not all risk is created equal. Because we continue to live in an unjust society, risk-taking can have different consequences for different people. What can be challenging and uncomfortable for some can be dangerous and life-changing for others. For many people, simply being themselves can be a risky act. Early childhood professionals have a responsibility to learn how racism and other inequities affect risk.

Exploring Pedagogical Practice: Questions to Explore Risk

Use some of the following questions to help you to think more about risk and risk competence in your work.

- Where in your life do you take risks? This can include physical risks but also emotional, intellectual, social, financial, and other risks.
- What kinds of risk-taking are you most comfortable with? What kinds of risks are more difficult for you? Why do you think that is?
- How does your relationship with risk affect the decisions you make in the classroom?
- What have you been able to learn or experience as a result of taking some kind of a risk?
- What is the difference between something that is challenging and something that is dangerous?
- How do you create safe spaces for others to practice taking risks?

RECAPPING THE ROLE OF THE PEDAGOGICAL LEADER TO SEE AND SUPPORT COMPETENCE IN CHILDREN AND ADULTS

Pedagogical leaders . . .

- See competence in themselves and others.
- Focus on strengths to build capacity rather than focusing on weaknesses.
- Support educators in exploring and reflecting on their own definition of competence.
- Seek to understand how our experiences influence our views of competence.
- Support children and adults in uncovering their unique gifts and passions.
- Explore ways that individuals can use their gifts within the program.
- Notice themselves and pay attention to their own judgments and assumptions.
- Focus on being curious and seeking to understand others' actions and ideas.
- Provide ways for educators to uncover their own curiosities.
- Help educators create questions as a lens to see competence in children and each other.
- Understand that what we give our energy and time to grows.
- Understand that we live in an unjust society, and risk-taking can have different consequences for different people.
- Understand that risk-taking happens in multiple ways, beyond physical risk.
- See the importance of building risk competence in children and adults.
- Invite educators to be observers of themselves.

CHAPTER FIVE

Pedagogical Leaders Support Learning in Multiple Ways by Design

"What could happen if we gave adult growth and learning the same diligent attention as we give child growth and learning?"

in conversation with pedagogical leader Margie Carter

Take a moment to consider . . .

What does professional learning mean to you?

In what ways do you learn best?

There is no doubt that the most valuable resource of any organization is people. The potential of human beings is immense. Yet none of us become masterful in our work by accident, and longevity in a job doesn't necessarily mean that someone is highly skilled. It requires intention, thoughtfulness, and a commitment to ongoing learning—and unlearning. It also requires that we offer time for professional learning to take place within our programs and organizations.

Unfortunately for many, there has been a narrow view of professional learning in the field of early education in North America. Traditionally, professional development opportunities, if they happen at all, have been designed around ideas that focus on quick fixes, consuming ideas for classroom activities, and external motivation. While all of these things can be helpful from time to time, it is extremely problematic when they become the foundation for professional learning.

The difficulty is that each of these approaches separates the educator from being an active participant in their own learning and teaches the educator to depend on someone else to do the thinking for them. Rather than building their own critical and innovative thinking, the educator can create the habit of looking to someone else to solve problems, gather information, or provide motivation. These approaches rob early learning professionals of the growth and satisfaction that comes when they have opportunities to think with others, consider their own experiences, experiment, research, reflect, and grow in their own self-awareness.

We know this because we were active participants in that traditional approach. Early in our careers, we spent hours offering workshops and training sessions that were naively designed to help educators fix the problems they faced in their classrooms and dole out a plethora of new things to try. We eagerly took up the role of the "sage on the stage" and handed out advice on everything from how to deal with difficult behaviors (in both children and adults) to how to organize activities and schedule time. Whenever there was a problem, we were called on to do a workshop as if it was our responsibility to offer some nugget of wisdom that would magically make the problem go away. It was an approach that focused more on problems than possibilities, and it was exhausting. And, of course, it didn't work. It took a few years to figure out, but thankfully, due to our own professional learning and the graciousness of some amazing mentors, we came to the realization that what we were doing was not always helpful. We had contributed to creating an environment that conveyed the idea that we knew best, and we unwittingly reinforced standardized responses that removed thinking and disempowered educators.

Thankfully, over the past twenty years we have released ourselves from the pressure to have the right answers and have embraced the beautiful complexity that comes with working together with other human beings. The problems we so desperately worked to solve early in our careers have become the gifts that help us learn more about ourselves and offer insight into our own practice and thinking. We have found that questions drive us more than answers, and we are energized by the understanding that our work is far more meaningful when it is informed by many different views and perspectives instead of a single narrative. Rather than questions that require quick, straightforward answers, like "What should I do?" "How do I do it?" or "Where do I get that?" we are more interested in thinking about questions that invite us to consider our own pedagogical practices. Questions like, "What is my responsibility here?" "What is informing my decision?" "Who can I think with about this?" and "What do I want to learn more about?" These types of questions ask something different of us and require that we redesign how we plan and organize professional learning experiences.

Thoughtfully constructed professional learning opportunities have the potential to transform how we work and think together as early learning professionals. They can also transform the way we live our lives. They can engage both the mind and the heart and open us up to exciting new ways to think about the purpose of education. When done well, professional learning helps disrupt old ways of thinking and can help advance the education system at large. In other words, professional development is a way to develop the profession as a whole. It is what ensures that we grow and move in response to what we are learning about our own practice, ourselves, and our histories, rather than simply following a set of imposed standards and policies. It is how practice and theory inform each other and how in turn they can inform policy. On top of all that, it can be enormously satisfying and inspiring.

Imagine thinking that an educator is just beginning their learning journey when they graduate with a teaching degree or diploma. What if the profession itself recognized a collective responsibility to continuously invest in the growth of educators and their leaders throughout their careers? What could happen if the need to have the right answer was replaced with the ability to ask important questions? Questions that create an eagerness to learn and help educators think more about why they do what they do, rather than how to do it? What if, instead of teaching techniques and strategies to deal with children, educators were given opportunities to nurture specific dispositions that could serve them and others in their work? How might things change if educators were liberated from working from one set of standardized practices and instead were exposed to many different ways of being and ways of knowing? What if documentation was seen as a useful learning tool rather than an obligatory practice used to assess children? Now imagine that instead of just trying to fit training sessions in on weekends or at the end of a long workday, professional learning was part of everyday practice, and performance reviews were replaced with learning plans. These are all things that we have seen happen when communities large and small rethink their approach to professional learning and invest in pedagogical leadership.

Part of this rethinking has to do with our approach and commitment to carving out time for individual and team meetings as well as for side by side work in the classroom. The truth is, time is a required investment for this work to happen, but having time alone doesn't necessarily create a culture of practice—it deeply matters how we use that time. We frequently hear two questions from both large organizations and small individual programs about how to do this work. The first is "How can we find the time?" and the second is "What are we supposed to do with this time?" Over the last twenty years we have studied ourselves and how our practices have evolved. We have witnessed firsthand the movement that happens when pedagogical leaders embed thinking structures and protocols into their practices. This chapter is dedicated to many different ways to use time. In it we explore ways to nurture learning communities, studying ourselves and the experiences that unfold in our classrooms. We offer you some ways to think about goals for learning together and also consider how the world around us can influence our pedagogical focuses. When it comes to evolving practices around professional learning, there are many things a pedagogical leader can do.

Pedagogical leaders . . .

- Nurture learning dispositions that are useful in practice.
- Understand that learning takes time.
- Support collaboration and perspective sharing.
- Use documentation and classroom research as a learning tool.
- Support educators in creating individual learning plans.
- Understand the most powerful learning happens side by side.
- Have clear pedagogical focuses to orient their work.

PEDAGOGICAL LEADERS NURTURE LEARNING DISPOSITIONS THAT ARE USEFUL IN PRACTICE

Now consider . . .

What are the characteristics you think are important for learning?

How do you nurture those characteristics in yourself?

Over the past several years we have seen increased opportunities for professional learning experiences that are designed to help early childhood educators acquire new knowledge and skills that can benefit their work with young children. While there is no doubt that educators need to have both knowledge and skill to do their work, the other important component to learning is disposition. Whereas knowledge refers to a person's theoretical understanding and skill considers a person's ability to apply that knowledge in practical ways, dispositions are about a person's natural inclination to behave in a particular way.

More simply put,

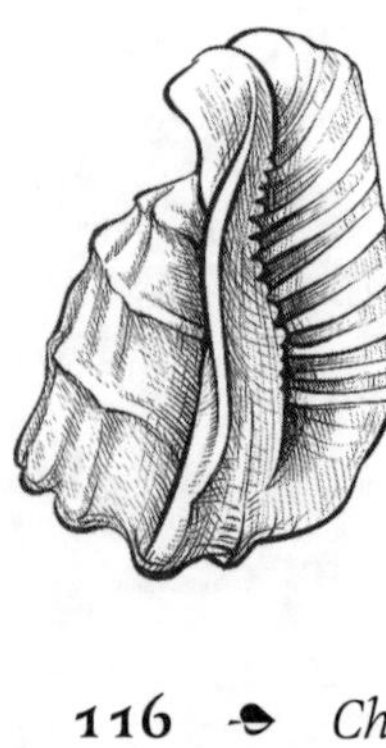

- Knowledge is about what we know.
- Skill is about what we can do.
- Disposition is about our tendency to do it.

We the authors were first introduced to the idea of disposition through the work of Dr. Lilian Katz, who wrote extensively about learning dispositions for children, describing them as "habits of mind" that influence teacher attitudes about—and reaction to—day-to-day interactions in early childhood settings. A person's disposition tends to shine through in their prevailing attitudes and the outlook they hold about life. For example, a person who always seems to be in a good mood might be referred to as having a sunny disposition. Likewise, a person who is known to take quick action might be thought of as having a disposition to be decisive, and a person who likes to win might be called competitive. We all have different ways of being that feel natural to us, and as we move through life, the behaviors and attitudes we carry with us shape our life experiences. Anne Marie's inclination to spend time in the garden led her to study herbalism, while Lorrie's fondness for being with people has resulted in her wide circle of close friendships. Dispositions like these are naturally nurtured in us over time through our relationships and experiences.

While we all have dispositions, they may or may not be useful in growing the kind of vibrant learning community you are hoping for. For this to happen, pedagogical leaders focus on nurturing specific learning dispositions that work in combination with skills and knowledge. As pedagogical leaders, we strive to nurture in ourselves the same learning dispositions that we want to support in the pedagogical leaders and educators around us. We want to work alongside educators who have dispositions to be curious and to question their own certainties. This means we create spaces that encourage people to ask questions and we release ourselves and them from the pressure to have all the right answers. We want to take up this work with people who are optimistic and hopeful for a better future, so we invite others to think about their hopes and dreams for their work as we share ours with them. Because we believe the work we are doing requires people to be reflective and thoughtful, creative and kind, collaborative and community minded, it is incumbent on us to create an environment for those ways of being to flourish.

We also want to acknowledge that these particular dispositions are not the only ways of being that are beneficial to learning communities. As we continue on our own learning journey, we find ourselves unpacking how our privilege and inherited narratives have influenced our ideas about the kinds of dispositions we believe are useful in our work. The truth is, there is room for many different ways of being. Perhaps embracing difference is one of the most valuable dispositions we can have.

When pedagogical leaders take time to notice and name the kinds of learning dispositions that are useful in their work, they can begin to create the conditions necessary to nurture them both in themselves and in others, even if these habits don't come naturally. In this same way, educators can notice and name the dispositions they want to bring to their classrooms. Listed here are some behaviors and attitudes that may be present when someone has particular learning dispositions.

Learning Disposition	The person you see . . .
Curiosity	▪ Is observant, with a longing to learn more about the people and the world around them ▪ Asks questions to seek clarity ▪ Accesses information in a variety of ways, such as reading and listening to others ▪ Seeks to understand rather than make assumptions and judgments
Collaboration	▪ Has an eagerness to work and think with others ▪ Shows a willingness to share ideas ▪ Sees value in sharing diverse perspectives and seeks out ideas that may be different than their own
Openness	▪ Has a willingness to question certainties ▪ Challenges common narratives and traditional approaches ▪ Sees value in having their ideas questioned and resists being defensive ▪ Remains open to different ways of being and understands that there isn't just one right way
Courageousness	▪ Demonstrates a willingness to take risks or make mistakes ▪ Shows an openness to experiment with different ideas and try new things ▪ Doesn't shy away from uncomfortable conversations and situations ▪ Understands that vulnerability is not weakness ▪ Has the courage to name and counter inequity
Self-Awareness	▪ Is willing to reflect on themselves and their practice ▪ Desires to understand more about their own thinking and feeling and why they respond in certain ways ▪ Understands their own values and beliefs ▪ Acknowledges that their behavior has impact and influence on others
Optimism	▪ Sees the strengths and competencies of others ▪ Believes in their ability to effect positive change ▪ Shows persistence and perseverance ▪ Works toward goals even in the face of challenges and setbacks ▪ Brings a sense of joy and hopefulness to their work

Pedagogical leaders understand the importance of developing intentional practices that nurture ways of being. Throughout this book you find many structures that can help nurture different learning dispositions. You may recall the story in the previous chapter of how pedagogical leader Judy supported a toddler team to create a question they could use as a lens to see competence. In using this structure Judy helped to nurture dispositions for curiosity, collaboration, and self-awareness. Consider how pedagogical leader Julie nurtures the disposition for reading within her program. Julie has always valued taking time to read as an important part of her work. As a child her love of reading was nurtured in her at home and she often found herself reading for the sheer pleasure of it. As a pedagogical leader she holds a strong belief that having the skill and knowledge to read is essential to our work together in early education. She believes that while having the skill and knowledge is essential, if a person doesn't have a disposition for reading, they are not truly a *reader.*

In her program Julie was noticing that educators displayed little desire to read. Although she was purchasing many new resource books and sending out articles, the educators were not engaging and she felt as though she was taking up all the reading on her own. In an effort to nurture a culture of reading, she decided to start small. She began collecting quotes and short statements to post in the staff room and even the staff washroom. In weekly team meetings and monthly staff meetings, she made a point of opening the meeting with a quote that linked to the ideas they were talking about. She invited the group to reflect on the quotes and share what stood out for them or how it got them thinking. Once this practice became embedded in their meetings, she began inviting educators to select the quote for the meetings. Slowly, she noticed how educators were becoming more eager to seek out quotes and more excited to share their findings in the meetings. As Judy noticed the increasing engagement, she began to look for short articles or pieces of articles to share with the group.

In these meetings Julie provided more time for reflecting on the articles and created more intentional ways to think about the articles and how they connected to values and practice. Over time, this desire to read and reflect together became part of the daily life of the program. It wasn't long before educators were selecting books they wanted to read together and took the time to read chapter by chapter, sharing stories of how the ideas connected and challenged their thinking.

Julie explored different protocols that they could use for reflection and began to adapt and create new structures of her own. Reading had become an important part of the culture of the program, and educators began to pay more attention to the books they were offering children. They started to think more critically about the messages and values that lay within the children's books and sought out books that aligned with the values they wanted to grow in their classrooms and removed those that did not. Pedagogical leaders understand that this work requires engagement and it takes time. When pedagogical leaders create structure to nurture dispositions, educators are more likely to nurture them in children.

Exploring Your Own Practice: Studying Text Together

Structures provided throughout this book can support teams in reflecting on reading. We have found the Final Word protocol one of the most useful tools for studying articles and books. The Final Word protocol was developed through the School Reform Initiative. The initiative hosts a website where you can find hundreds of protocols (www.schoolreforminitiative.org). Over the years we have adapted and massaged many protocols and structures to best fit with our work. We encourage you to do the same with the structures we offer you throughout this book.

Consider an article or book you would like to explore with your teams, and decide together how much the group will read ahead of the meeting and how much time you will dedicate to the study. You will notice that this structure offers times for each section. We have found this to be an important aspect of this structure.

"Using this protocol for reflecting on articles and books for book studies has been helpful. I find that it focuses the discussion and ensures everyone participating has a voice and provides the group with an opportunity to listen. Slowing down the process of reflection guides us to reflect on other perspectives and gives us new ways of seeing each other and seeing children."

Paola, pedagogical leader

Adapted Final Word Protocol—A Process for Studying Text

1. Each participant writes a short reflection on the big ideas from the book that resonate with them. What new understandings have surfaced? What questions are still lingering? (3–4 min.)
2. The presenter describes their reflections and shares their new understandings and questions. (3 min.)
3. The group has the chance to ask probing or clarifying questions and share their reflections. (3–5 min.)
4. The presenter responds. (1 min.)
5. Repeat.
6. Final reflections: What common threads and big ideas resonate with the group? (3–5 min.)

www.schoolreforminitiative.org/protocols

The structure of this protocol provides each individual with the opportunity to share ideas and perspectives. It can sometimes feel a bit bumpy at the beginning, and we have noticed that educators who like to talk a lot sometimes struggle to give up the floor to others at first. This structure really lends itself to the practice of reflecting and also encourages listening to others. By holding to allotted times, we find that it provides the group with a disciplined way both to reflect and to listen. The role of the pedagogical leader is to allow time for each participant to present their reflections, have the group share their thinking, and ask the presenter questions about what they have heard or are thinking about. As the group size may vary, consider the amount of time needed to allow participants to fully move through the structure. The process is one way to grow a disposition for reading while at the same time nurturing reflective thinking and listening.

Exploring Your Own Practice: Consider Specific Ways to Nurture Dispositions

Here are some of the dispositions we have come to know as useful in our practice. However, we understand that there are many others. You can use this structure to think with others about these or other dispositions that you feel are useful. Consider specific ways you might nurture these in both adults and children.

Learning Disposition	How can I nurture these dispositions in myself?	How can I nurture these dispositions in educators?	How can educators nurture these dispositions in children?
Curiosity			
Collaboration			
Openness			
Courageousness			
Self-Awareness			
Optimism			

www.redleafpress.org/crp/d-9.pdf

"Collaborating with others is vital to my work. I am just one person with one set of lived experiences. While my experiences may be diverse, my perception of them never changes, as I'm always the one filtering and interpreting what I am exposed to. Coming together with others and listening to their interpretations and experiences in this world reshapes how I am able to perceive what happens around me and in me. It opens my eyes to new possibilities and invites me to compose new meaning. Collaboration changes me daily. Keeps me thinking."

Renee, pedagogical leader

As the landscape in early childhood continues to evolve and change, early childhood educators may very well find that the kind of work being asked of them today is different from when they started their career. Pedagogical leaders can help by offering experiences and engaging with educators in ways that nurture the learning dispositions required for today's early childhood classrooms.

This book is layered with stories and structures that nurture many of the dispositions we have described here. As you read through, look to see where you notice specific dispositions being nurtured and consider what structures best support what you are trying to grow in your program. Understand that this growth depends on having systems and structures that allow for time, practice, and constant attention.

PEDAGOGICAL LEADERS UNDERSTAND THAT LEARNING TAKES TIME

Now consider . . .

What have you noticed about how your thinking has grown and evolved over time?

How do you reflect on and revisit your learning?

Over the thirty-five years that we authors have been in the early education field, we have seen many changes in both the approaches to professional learning as well as the amount of opportunities offered to educators. It was once thought that when you received your diploma or degree in early childhood education, your learning was finished. There may have been one or two training opportunities offered each year, and finding resources that went beyond offering ideas for songs, art activities, and fingerplays was difficult at best. Often there was only one annual conference where early childhood educators gathered, attending workshops to take home a pocketful of ideas and strategies ranging from behavior management to circle time songs and stories. Fortunately, as our field has evolved we have come to better understand how learning happens for both children and adults. Professional learning opportunities have multiplied in number, and the kinds of sessions offered have also changed. But not all professional learning is created equal. If we want to create a culture of professional learning that grows our profession and creates a culture of reflective practice, we have to develop ways of offering learning opportunities that don't look for quick fixes or strategies but rather move us from training to thinking. Pedagogical leaders also understand that this type of learning together takes time. The role of the pedagogical leader is to organize space and time for educators to reflect on their practice, dig more deeply into new ideas, and make intentional decisions. Pedagogical leaders understand that taking a workshop or reading an article isn't going to change practice. It is only when we have opportunities to reflect on our learning and revisit our ideas over time that we see a real shift. Read how pedagogical leader Tracy used an article to delve into classroom practice and engage educators over time.

Tracy worked hard to stay connected to the latest research on early learning and development and recently came across an article by Tom Drummond, "Enterprise Talk" (n.d.). The article speaks of the authenticity and power of language and how, as early childhood educators, we can use our interactions to nurture and grow dispositions such as empathy, curiosity, and perseverance. It offers educators a way to reconsider how they use questions, praise, and directions in the classroom. Our language is a way to nurture our values. Knowing the educators in the preschool room had just finished naming their classroom values, Tracy felt this article would be a great way to think with educators and deepen their practice.

She shared the article with the preschool team and asked if they would like to study it together. They eagerly accepted and agreed to read it ahead of their next team meeting. When they met together, Tracy facilitated the meeting using three questions to guide their dialogue.

What really resonated with you in the article?

What does it have you thinking about in your own practice?

What do you want to learn more about?

These three questions sparked lively conversations, and over the next several weeks the educators began to practice the ideas in the article. The article challenges educators to stop asking questions as a way to manage behavior, stop praising children for what they do, and stop giving directions. Instead, it asks educators to notice and narrate what they see and offer honest recognition rather than praise. In their next team meeting, the educators spoke of how difficult it was to shift their practice in this way, but they were noticing subtle changes in the group. The children seemed to be staying longer in play, there was a deeper sense of pride when children were noticed for their actions, and there seemed to be less conflict.

While the educators continued to practice these ideas, the pedagogical leader asked them to read the article again and at their next team meeting offered a new way to think through it. This time each person was asked to write a short reflection on the article and consider:

What new understandings do you have?

What questions are still lingering?

What is new that stood out for you that you hadn't noticed before?

Once they shared their reflections, the other team members were invited to ask each other clarifying and probing questions and reflect on how each other's ideas were influencing their thinking.

Moving back into the classroom to continue practicing this new way of being with children, the educator team had a deeper understanding of each other and what they were trying to grow in themselves and the children. Over time, the educators began to feel more comfortable using the guides of enterprise talk, and they could feel a shift in the culture of the classroom. The values they wanted to grow had become a focus, and they called attention to when they saw the children living in them.

At the next team meeting, Tracy again brought them back to the article, this time asking each educator to highlight

- a sentence that was meaningful to you and helped you gain a deeper understanding of the text;
- a phrase that moved, engaged, provoked, or challenged you; and
- a word that captured your attention or struck you as powerful.

The team then shared their responses, and Tracy offered the following questions to dig deeper:

> How do your choices connect with your values as individuals and as a team?
>
> What did you learn about yourself through this exercise?
>
> What did you learn about each other?

Each time the team met to revisit the article and delve into it in different ways, their understanding grew, not just of the practice of enterprise talk, but of each other and the kind of classroom culture they were trying to create.

Pause and Reflect

How do you slow down and reflect on your learning?

What have you noticed when you revisit an article or book you have read before?

The number of articles, resources, and workshops available to us today can sometimes feel overwhelming. We can choose to collect and consume ideas, or we can take time to reflect more deeply on them over time, even over months or years. Many years ago, one of our mentors suggested that each year we go back and reread a book or piece of writing that we feel had an impact on our work. In this way, she suggested, we could regularly revisit ideas with fresh eyes. What we notice in this revisiting is that as we grow and evolve in our thinking, we discover new meanings in the ideas and concepts these books and writings offer. Revisiting ideas over time can provide an opportunity to reinterpret and rethink, consider new questions, and build on prior understandings. When pedagogical leaders find ways to revisit ideas with educators, it provides them opportunities to practice the concepts they are learning about and notice how they translate into their daily practice. When pedagogical leaders give time to educators to reflect throughout the process, the educators can begin to see how their thinking has evolved over time and see for themselves the importance of slowing down.

"Working alongside a pedagogical leader has shown how being disciplined in reflective thinking about my practice can shift the way I move in the classroom. When we embrace the complexities of our work and stay with the tensions that arise, it can create space for rich, meaningful experiences with children."

Charlotte, educator

Exploring Pedagogical Practice: Studying Written Material Together Over Time

Consider a book, article, or piece of documentation you would like to explore more deeply with your team over time. Using the same questions from the previous story, notice how each of the sets of questions gives shape to the conversations, and notice how the questions begin to shift practice.

Beginning

Consider with the team what ideas they would like to explore. Prepare ahead of time with the readings, and set aside time to meet with educators to explore these questions.

- What really resonated with you in the article?
- What does it have you thinking about in your own practice?
- What do you want to learn more about?

Digging Deeper

Take some time at the beginning of your pedagogical meeting to reflect on what the team is noticing in themselves and their practice. Invite each person to write a short reflection on the work and consider the following:

- What new understandings do you have?
- What questions are still lingering?
- What is new that stood out for you that you hadn't noticed before?

Invite educators to ask each other probing and clarifying questions to support them to fill out their ideas and thinking.

(Adapted from the Final Word protocol from School Reform Initiative)

Deconstructing Language and Values

Invite the team to move deeper into the work, looking closely at the words that resonate with them. The key in this moment is to dig into why:

- a sentence was meaningful to you and helped you gain a deeper understanding of the text
- a phrase moved, engaged, provoked, or challenged you
- a word captured your attention or struck you as powerful

Once the team has shared responses, take some time to reflect on the common threads and the values that are coming up from their reflections.

- How do your choices and reasoning connect with your values as individuals and a team?
- What did you learn about yourself through this exercise?
- What did you learn about each other?

www.redleafpress.org/crp/d-10.pdf

PEDAGOGICAL LEADERS SUPPORT COLLABORATION AND PERSPECTIVE SHARING

Now consider . . .

In what ways do you collaborate with others?

How do you respond to people who have a different perspective than you?

There is no denying that each one of the more than seven billion people on this planet are gloriously different. Each of us has our own way of being and thinking based on our lived experience, personality, and personal point of view. While we often find and even seek out others who share similar perspectives, we will never find anyone who is exactly the same. We are not supposed to be. Even children from the same family with the same parents and upbringing can turn out to be vastly different from one another. It is through our differences that we are able to consider experiences other than our own and expand our understanding of the world. Understanding differences helps people develop a greater appreciation for each other while breaking down barriers. However, this is not always an easy task. Hearing different perspectives sometimes can make people feel defensive. Others may feel like their way of thinking is wrong and needs to change. Particularly for groups of people who have been historically marginalized, it is not always safe to share perspectives.

> *"Thinking together with my pedagogical leader has helped me to dive below the surface and see the bigger concepts that are present. She challenges my thinking by offering questions from perspectives I hadn't thought of to expand my thought process and deepen my understanding."*
>
> ~ *Jen, educator*

While many people would agree that hearing a different perspective is a good thing, in reality, being open enough to allow other viewpoints to actually affect how we think can be difficult. It is important for pedagogical leaders to embrace the differences that individuals can bring and create respectful and safe spaces for multiple ways of thinking and knowing to exist and grow together. Successful collaboration requires being open to different perspectives as well as an understanding that there is a distinct difference between working from shared values and common goals and getting everyone to think the same way. Pedagogical leaders can encourage individuals to bring themselves, their ideas, and their own understanding to a group by encouraging dialogue about differences and creating a culture where difference is expected. They can set up intentional spaces that bring people together who have different ideas or lived experiences and help facilitate respectful conversations. Pedagogical leaders help build trust when they show interest in people, ask how they are doing, and thank them for having courage to share. When this happens, there are much higher levels of engagement, innovation, and feelings of belonging. The group itself shifts, becoming more inclusive and open to new ways of thinking as members consider other points of view.

A great example of this can be seen in this conversation about identity. The educators had established a practice of creating identity panels for every child in their classroom, including things like the child's name, family structure, gender, and culture. One of the educators in the group raised the concern that creating panels in this way felt like they were tokenizing the idea of identity. She shared her perspective that identities are complex and simply creating a panel that answered a couple of questions about a child didn't really help them think deeply about the children as individuals. Everyone in the group agreed. Then she said, "A child's name is just surface. It doesn't really tell you anything about who they are." This comment elicited a myriad of responses from her colleagues who had very different perspectives. One brought up birth stories and the different ways that parents approach naming children. One shared what she had been learning about children who have changed their names because of frequent mispronunciation or in order to assimilate into a world set up to advantage white English-speaking people.

Pause and Reflect

In what ways do you as a pedagogical leader seek out perspectives that are different than your own?

In what ways do you or might you create a space for others to share perspectives that are different than your own?

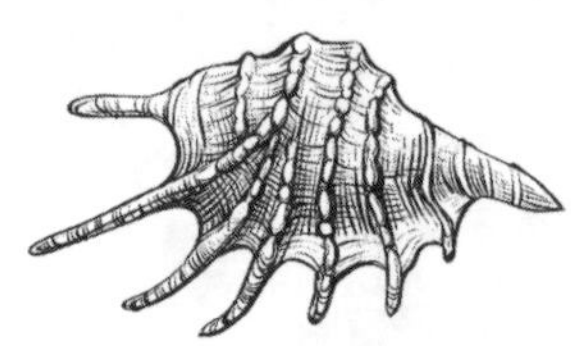

This group of educators had a shared value of honoring individual identities, yet their understanding and personal experiences around identity were very different. As they listened to each other, the group began to shift its collective understanding of *identity*. As a result, they started to question their own certainties on the subject and were inspired to think more about where identity comes from, how it changes over time, and what kinds of things influence a person's identity. Conversations like this are generative in nature as they help groups of people construct new understandings and perspectives as they listen to one another. They help complexify ideas and show that there is rarely one right way to think about something. Generative conversations require people to release their need for certainty. They help us dig into ideas, challenge what we think we know, and consciously seek out different perspectives. They require that we resist defending our own ideas at the expense of others, and they challenge assumptions and uncover biases. They help individuals and groups come to new understandings that are impossible alone. Creating space for generative conversations disrupts the idea that one person is the keeper of information. The idea that the leader is the one with the right answers is long past. Everyone's voice matters and indeed is necessary. Real change happens when there is collective meaning making and when action becomes shared. A useful way to create a space for generative conversations to take place is to think with the Three Fields of Knowledge. The three fields of knowledge move through a process that considers how we learn from, with, and on behalf of one another.

Three Fields of Knowledge

What do we know?	What is known?	What new knowledge is possible?
The ideas and knowledge that are shared by participants involved in the discussion.	The knowledge of theory, research, best practices, and the perspectives of those outside of the group.	The knowledge that we can cocreate through our collaborative work and new understandings.
Adaptive learning: The sharing from participants reshapes what is known and understood.	Additional learning: Adding to what is already known.	Creative and innovative learning: Discovering new meaning and new ways of thinking and taking action.

Karen Carter, Chris Cotton, and Kirsten Hill. 2009. "Network Facilitation: The Power of Protocols." National College for School Leadership, UK. https://citeseerx.ist.psu.edu/viewdoc/download?doi=10.1.1.617.4508&rep=rep1&type=pdf.

"Collaboration with others moves me beyond my own thinking and understanding; it has pushed me to explore other perspectives, to practice listening with the intention to better understand, to practice being a critical friend, to be OK with not having the answers, to be curious. I am the educator I am today predominantly due to the educators I have had the privilege of working alongside throughout my journey. We inspire each other."

Julie, pedagogical leader

Using the Three Fields of Knowledge to Support Generative Thinking

As a pedagogical leader it is important to support the kinds of moving conversations that leave groups thinking a little differently at the end of a discussion than they did at the beginning. Understanding what each of the three fields of knowledge look and feel like can help us consciously create the kinds of generative conversations that help evolve thinking and practice.

First Field: Practitioner Knowledge	**What does a first field of knowledge conversation look like?**
This is the personal and subjective knowledge that each of us constructs through our individual lived experiences and understandings of the world. While we often find others who have similar understandings on some topics, we will never find another person who shares exactly the same understanding on everything. Entering conversations from the first field of knowledge means sharing what you know and understand and why you feel that way. It is how each of us can offer our own perspective on things and is an important starting point for a generative conversation. However, conversations that stay in the first field don't shift or expand anyone's thinking.	Everyone shares their personal perspective on something, but no one walks away thinking any differently. What I offer in a discussion might help someone recall their own experience or remember something that they already know, but it does not make them reconsider or think more deeply about an idea. "I might know what you think, but I haven't changed the way I think."

Second Field: Public Knowledge	What does a second field of knowledge conversation look like?
This is knowledge offered by others, particularly knowledge gained through research or acknowledged best practice. Entering conversations from the second field of knowledge means exploring and being open to new ideas or interpretations that can either build on or challenge our personal understandings.	A group brings curiosity and questions to explore a topic, often thinking with resources such as articles, books, lectures, podcasts, documentaries, exhibits, and so on. Ideas that are shared reach beyond the people in the discussion and consider insights and perspectives that offer new information and invite different considerations. "I am aware that this is a new idea for me, and I am open to learning more about it."
Third Field: New Knowledge This is the new knowledge created within us when the first two fields of knowledge combine through collaborative inquiry. Ranging from tiny to mammoth, these are the shifts we make in our thinking as a result of combining our own understandings with that of others.	**What does a third field of knowledge conversation look like?** Conversations are generative, and ideas grow off each other. There is an expansion of new ideas and questions and an awareness that our thinking is starting to change and new ways of thinking are emerging. "What I am learning is helping me think differently than I did before. I have a different understanding and new questions."

Consider these additional tips for creating generative dialogues.

- Be open to ideas that are different from your own.
- Be willing to share what you think and why.
- Listen to others with curiosity.
- Ask questions.
- Resist drawing conclusions.

Pause and Reflect

How do you know when a conversation is generative?

Layering Voices: A Structure for Collaborative Writing and Generating Ideas

Not all conversations are generative. Sometimes people can talk for hours, repeating the same ideas over and over again in different ways. Using the three fields of knowledge as a guide can help pedagogical leaders and educators learn to recognize when their conversations are circling around things they already know and when they are moving and growing, bringing in different perspectives and offering new considerations. Another way to create an opportunity for generative conversations that bring in multiple perspectives is through a pedagogical documentation process we call Layering Voices. Layering Voices works by offering an initial provocation and then invites one or more people to respond by layering or adding their perspectives in a particular way. We originally developed this particular structure in response to a phenomenon we observed with educator documentation. We noticed that while many educators had taken up the practice of photographing and writing about children's experiences, they were doing it in isolation. We also noticed that they were feeling a pressure to produce complete polished pieces of writing. Our goal was to liberate educators from this fast-moving approach to producing documentation and instead invite them to practice using their observations as a catalyst to think with others.

The Layering Voices structure helps educators and pedagogical leaders build on each other's ideas and leaves a visible trail of how thinking unfolds. It often starts with one person offering a piece of writing about something they experienced in the classroom that is impactful for them in some way. This piece of writing is then offered to another person to read and respond to with any new or different ideas it conjured up for them. A third person then reads both pieces of writing and writes down what comes to mind for them, layering their ideas on top of the first two. The point is not to critique or correct but to build on what has been offered, coming at it from different points of view and generating new ideas. Layering Voices exercises can help educators see how their ideas can launch new conversations. Educators practice using documentation as a collaborative thinking tool to construct new meaning and create fuller understandings of their work. Watch how these educators use the Layering Voices approach to build on each other's thinking and start to reveal the complexities that exist in a simple moment.

Initial Offering: Charlotte

Brody picked a dandelion, closed his eyes, and blew the seeds. He then let out a big belly laugh, and I couldn't help but laugh along with him. This encounter left me thinking more about the organic experiences children have and what happens when we notice the extraordinary within the ordinary. I find myself wondering how doing this can help us think differently about relationships and deepen our connections with each other and the earth.

Layering Voice: Lindsay

I am continuously amazed by children's innate connection to the earth, the way in which they encounter their world with wonder, curiosity, and joy. This experience with Brody has me thinking about the way of being that we want to nurture in relation to the earth. One in which we notice and slow down and give attention to the other living things that exist here. What is it about dandelions that draw children in, and how might we pay attention to them differently? How might giving our time and attention to the "ordinary" things and ordinary moments continue to nurture a different relationship with the earth—a relationship in which dandelions are more than just a weed?

Layering Voice Two: Renee

I've been reading a book called *Braiding Sweetgrass* by Robin Wall Kimmerer. Her writing is teaching me to keep learning about what it truly means for a human being to live in reciprocity with the more-than-human world around us. This is the first thing that jumped into my head when I read about Body's encounter with the dandelion. I find myself thinking about what the dandelion was doing before Brody picked it. Where were those seeds going to end up before his breath blew them into the wind? What will happen to the plant when the fun of picking and blowing is over? Will Brody remember the dandelion for the joy it gifted him? When do we as human beings start to harness the belief that the natural world around us is ours for the taking? As educators, what is our responsibility to nurture a different kind of relationship with the world we share with other living beings? How can we build reciprocal relationships with the more-than-human world that honor both the life and the memory of all that we encounter?

Layering Voices allows educators and pedagogical leaders to use writings and other provocations to think about and generate new ideas together. Exercises like this one intentionally create space for different ways of thinking and reveal nuanced complexities within educators' work.

Exploring Pedagogical Practice: Collaboration and Perspective Sharing

Layering Voices can start in different ways. An initial offering might be a documented moment in a classroom, but it can also be a poem, a quote, a part or full article, or some other written provocation to start ideas rolling around a particular topic of interest.

Practice with a colleague layering your voice on the following quote from the book *Braiding Sweetgrass: Indigenous Wisdom, Scientific Knowledge, and the Teachings of Plants* by Robin Wall Kimmerer: "Knowing that you love the earth changes you, activates you to defend and protect and celebrate. But when you feel that the earth loves you in return, that feeling transforms the relationship from a one-way street into a sacred bond" (2015, 124–25).

Layering Voice:

- What comes to mind for you as you read this quote?
- What themes or ideas do you see being played with here?
- How might those themes or ideas relate to your own work?

Layering Voice Two:

- What ideas come up for you as you read both this quote and the first response?
- How did the first response influence how you interpret the quote?
- Do you see any different themes or ideas being played with here?
- How do you relate what you just read to your work?

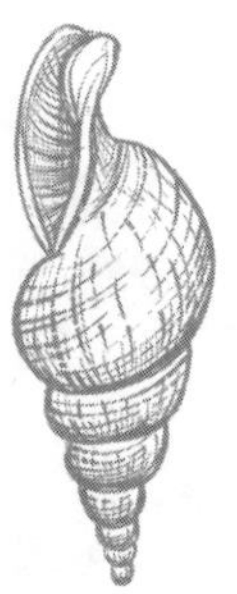

Now that you have practiced with the quote above, consider using this structure to generate a conversation about a moment in a classroom, a photograph, an article, or a podcast of interest.

Layering Voice One: This person reads, listens to, or watches what has been offered and writes down what comes to mind for them. Questions to spur thinking include:

- How does what you just read resonate with what you know or believe?
- Does it bring up any particular emotion for you and why?
- Does it make you question what you know or believe in any way?
- What different thoughts come up for you as you think along with what was offered?

Layering Voice Two: This person reads, listens to, or watches the original provocation as well as the first person's response. They then respond in writing to what comes to mind for them after reading the first person's response.

- What comes to mind for you after reading the first response?
- Does any of what you just read resonate with what you know or believe?
- Does it bring up any particular emotion for you and why?
- Does it make you question what you know or believe in any way?
- What different thoughts come up for you as you think along with what was offered?

Acknowledge new ideas and questions: Reflect on your writing as a group. Try to identify any specific shifts in thinking. Notice any challenges that this conjures up for you, and consider any new questions that might lead you to new resources and perspectives.

PEDAGOGICAL LEADERS USE DOCUMENTATION AND CLASSROOM RESEARCH AS A LEARNING TOOL

Now consider . . .

How do you use documentation in your work?

The idea of using documentation to support learning is fast becoming the norm in many early learning environments across North America. Schools in places like Reggio Emilia in Italy, Aotearoa New Zealand, and other parts of the world have demonstrated the richness that documentation can offer and the value it can bring to early learning classrooms. While there is no doubt that many educators find documentation to be a valuable tool, there are many others for whom it just feels like a chore added to their very busy day. For still others, it feels like an overwhelming struggle to even know how to start.

Often documentation is used as a tool to highlight and assess children's development. It is produced as a way to prove that children are learning something. In response to the challenges that many educators feel around documentation, many computerized programs are available to help make the process seem faster and easier. For a nominal fee and access to a little technology, educators can click a button, insert a photo, choose from a selection of comments or developmental stages, and presto—their daily documentation is complete and sent off to families. While we agree that some technologies can be helpful in communicating with families or sharing stories of daily experiences, they do not typically engage educators in thinking deeply about their practice.

As pedagogical leaders we are interested in how we can use documentation to help us engage in a process of learning with others. Consider how documentation can help create greater understanding of our own thinking, illuminate new ideas, generate new questions, and assist us in our own professional learning. When you think about it, you can learn a great deal about yourself by reading your own documentation. It highlights your perspective about something or someone. It gives visibility to what is important to you at that moment and reveals your values, understandings, and beliefs.

There are many fine books and resources available that are dedicated solely to pedagogical documentation. For the purposes of our work here, we want to offer a couple of specific ways that pedagogical leaders can practice using documentation as a professional learning tool with educators to study and learn more about both children's thinking and their own.

Studying Children's Photos Together

Taking photos has become a more common practice in many early learning classrooms. Technology has afforded us the opportunity to take hundreds of photos, delete those we don't need, and save, store, or print the ones that we do. Programs often share photos on their walls or in journals. Photos can also be a powerful tool for understanding and making meaning of thinking, for both adults and children. Pedagogical leaders can take up the practice of using photos as a way to study children. One of the structures we have found that supports this careful looking is the Visible Thinking protocol, See, Think, Wonder.

The practice of studying photos is just that, a practice. While the thinking routine is quite simple in its format, the role of the pedagogical leader is to help educators stay in each layer of the routine so they really explore all of the nuances in a photo. This careful looking provides space for thoughtful interpretations and can stimulate curiosity.

See, Think, Wonder

What do you see?

At this stage in the process, pedagogical leaders invite educators to make observations rather than interpretations. The act of carefully looking requires us to slow down and see the details in an image. When we tease out the details of an image, it gives us clues to the story inside. When we can look together with others, we see more and we build a deeper understanding of the image.

What do you see?

What stands out to you?

What do you think about that?

Now educators take their careful observations and consider what they think may be going on in the image and why they think that is so. Making meaning is an important step in moving our practice forward. When we consider our own theories and those of others, it influences our responses and the questions that move us.

What do you think is happening?

What makes you say that?

What do you wonder?

The final layer in this thinking process is to provoke new curiosities and questions that educators can take back into the classroom. It provides a new lens to explore, respond to, and build a culture of thinking.

What does this make you wonder?

What questions come up for you from your careful looking?

This thinking routine was developed as part of the Visible Thinking project at Project Zero, Harvard Graduate School of Education.

You can use the next photo to practice or invite educators to choose one or two photos from their collection. With the dozens of photos educators often take each day, narrowing down to one or two can be difficult. It may help to consider which photos best connect to a story, a relationship, or a moment in time.

Our days are busy and children move quickly, so taking photos and taking the time to deeply study them helps educators slow down, reflect, and make meaning in the moments in their days. The Thinking Lens® is another powerful protocol we use to study photos and videos alongside educators. Developed by Deb Curtis, Margie Carter, and Ann Pelo, the Thinking Lens® invites us to look carefully, using detailed questions to guide the conversation. It helps us reflect on our own thinking, the perspectives of others, the competencies of children, the physical and social and emotional environment, and how our reflections can influence our responses.

"Studying documentation with others has helped me see children in a whole new way. Coming from a theme-based childcare center, that was all I knew, and studying documentation opened my eyes to see that children are doing so much more than playing. They are testing theories, questioning the world, and trying to understand it. Even now in more of a pedagogical leadership role, I see myself learning things about children each and every time I study a new piece of documentation with educators and artists."

~ Vicky, pedagogical leader

A Thinking Lens® for Reflection and Inquiry

Knowing Yourself

What captures my attention as children engage, explore, and interact? Why?

What delights me as I watch and listen?

What in my background and values is influencing my response to this situation and why?

What adult perspectives (standards, health and safety, time, goals) are on my mind?

Finding the Details of Children's Competencies That Engage Your Heart and Mind

What do I notice in the children's faces and actions?

Where do I see examples of children's strengths and competencies?

What do I think is valuable about this experience?

Seeking the Child's Point of View

What is the child drawn to and excited about?

What might the child be trying to accomplish?

Why might the child be interacting with others this way?

What developmental themes, ideas, or theories might the child be exploring?

Examining the Physical and Social and Emotional Environment

How is the organization and use of the physical space and materials affecting this situation?

How could we strengthen relationships here?

How are schedules and routines influencing this experience?

Considering Multiple Perspectives

How might the child's culture and family background be influencing this situation?

What questions might we ask to get the perspective of the child's family?

Who else or what other perspectives should we consider?

Who is represented, and who is missing?

What child development or early learning theories should we consider in this experience?

What desired early learning outcomes do I see reflected here?

Considering Opportunities and Possibilities for Next Steps

What values, philosophy, or desired outcomes do I want to influence my response?

What new or existing relationships could be strengthened?

Which learning goals could be a focus here?

What other materials and activities could be offered to build on this experience?

What new vocabulary could we begin to use?

Look at how questions from the Thinking Lens® can be used and adapted to study an image of children as well as an environment.

Know Yourself

- What captures my attention as the children engage, explore, and interact? Why?
- What in my background and values is influencing my response to this situation and why?

Find the Details of Children's Competence

- What do I notice in the children's faces and actions?
- What words of competence come to mind for me as I study this photo?

Seek the Child's Point of View

- What might the child be trying to accomplish?
- What ideas or theories might the child be exploring here?

Opportunities and Possibilities

- What values, philosophy, or desired outcomes do I want to influence my response?
- What other materials and activities could be offered to build on this experience?

Know Yourself

- What captures my attention and why?
- How are my values and background influencing my response?

Find the Details of Competence

- What do I notice about the organization and use of space and materials?
- How might relationships be strengthened here?

Consider Multiple Perspectives

- How might families respond to this space?
- What desired early learning outcomes do I see reflected here?

Opportunities and Possibilities

- What other materials and activities could be offered to build on this experience?
- What questions come up for me as I explore this image?

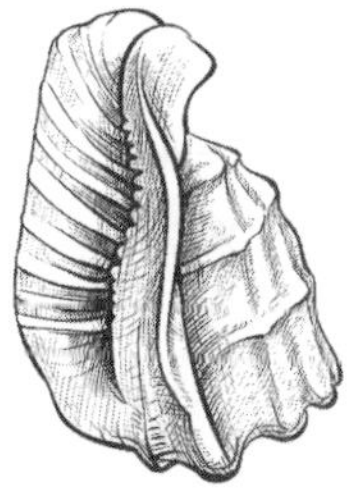

Collaborative Meaning Making

Reflecting on the details that photos offer can help educators construct a deeper understanding of the richness in children's experiences. Together with others you can consider what an experience might be like for a child and examine the many different ways children reveal their competence. Studying captured moments can help you remember what it is like to be a child and perhaps help you recall meaningful experiences from your own childhood. When educators allow themselves to stay present and linger in the beauty of a single moment it can be a reminder of the powerful role they have in shaping children's experiences. Children can remind us of our own humanity in a powerful way if we let them. In the following photo study a pedagogical leader brought a small group of educators together over several weeks to study children's photographs and embark on some collective writing.

Each week a different educator offered up an image of a child for the group to study together. Rather than moving through images quickly, they took thirty minutes to study each image and used a protocol to guide them. When they drifted their gaze or stopped talking, the pedagogical leader asked questions to help them look deeper into the photo. It was challenging, but as they stuck with it they began to realize that the more they looked, the more they saw. They studied details closely and imagined what the experience might have been like for the child. Different words came to mind as they continued to describe what they saw and felt. They reflected on the words they offered each other, considering their meaning and importance. As they studied the images and shared ideas, the pedagogical leader documented their conversation. Together they drew on their own conversations to do some collective writing on each photo.

Photo Study: Mason and the Tree

Inspired words: Close, curious, perspective, intimacy, inhale, discovery, contact, trust, focus

Some captured ideas: A conscious, gentle, purposeful gesture. How much time does it take to know a tree? What is there to learn in its crevices? Intimacy takes time. What must this encounter be like for the tree? To feel the warmth of a breath on a cool day. What kind of intimate knowledge does the tree offer to a face, hands, arms, and body? To lips? As adults we make assumptions about trees. We think we know that spring brings new life to the tree and that in autumn the leaves fall, but if we have never put our lips, nose, or chin gently on a tree, do we really know trees at all? This photo reminds me of trees that I have known, trees that I have swung from, eaten from, cradled my body in, trees of my childhood, long-forgotten trees.

The ideas became a collective piece of writing:

I remember that feeling . . .

A personal encounter that creates such an intimate relationship. The damp, pungent taste of a tree that fills me with knowing.

I remember those moments . . .

When there were no barriers to my connections

When I felt such trust that I could use the sensitivity of my own lips to aid in my discovery

I remember that understanding . . .

That we belong together—the earth and me

How grateful I am that you help me go to that place of remembering.

This different kind of photo study experience offered several things for the educators. It helped them to slow down and appreciate the value of being present in a moment. It reminded them of how much can be missed when we rush children. It offered them a way to study a child while bringing themselves personally into the moment. It helped them to remember their own intimate experiences with the world. It gave them an opportunity to explore their own values and demonstrated the power of language in shaping children's views. It provided them an opportunity to construct new meanings by building on each other's ideas. It gave them an experience in collective writing and enabled them to see how documentation can be used in different ways.

Try using this structure to guide you through a collaborative photo study and do some collective writing of your own.

Choose an image: It should capture an authentic moment that the child is experiencing. It should not be posed or planned.

Set an extended time for looking: The idea here is to practice looking closely, allowing the smallest details to offer information, elicit emotion, and inspire thinking. Allow yourself a minimum of ten minutes. With practice and planning you can increase your time. Consider the following prompts and questions to guide your looking.

Describe what you see.

What do you think this child might be experiencing here?

What clues does the photo offer that would make you say that?

What details do you notice in the child's face, hands, and body?

What is happening around the child that might have an impact on the child's experience?

Describe any emotions that this might bring up for you.

What word would you use to describe this moment? Why?

Can you relate personally to what this child might be experiencing here?

What memories does it bring up for you?

How does reflecting on this moment in this way affect you personally?

What does this image make you think about your own practice?

Studying Children's Drawings Together

While each of these structures have been offered here as a way to study images, by playing around with them a little you can also use them to think about other forms of documentation, including children's drawings.

There is something magical about children's drawings. Making marks on paper seems to be a natural activity that young children find pleasurable. These marks provide educators insight into children's joys and fears and can help reveal their personalities. Too often children's drawings aren't valued until they learn to draw something that is recognizable to an adult. Strokes and marks tend to be taken less seriously than stick people and suns. Yet we have learned that marks carry meaning and do have value, even if that value is the pleasure of listening to the sound that a pencil makes when it scratches against the paper. While we can never really know for sure what is going on inside a child's mind, we do think that studying children's drawings can offer us insight into who they are, what they know, and how they might be thinking and feeling. Consider this drawing from two-and-a-half-year-old Rika.

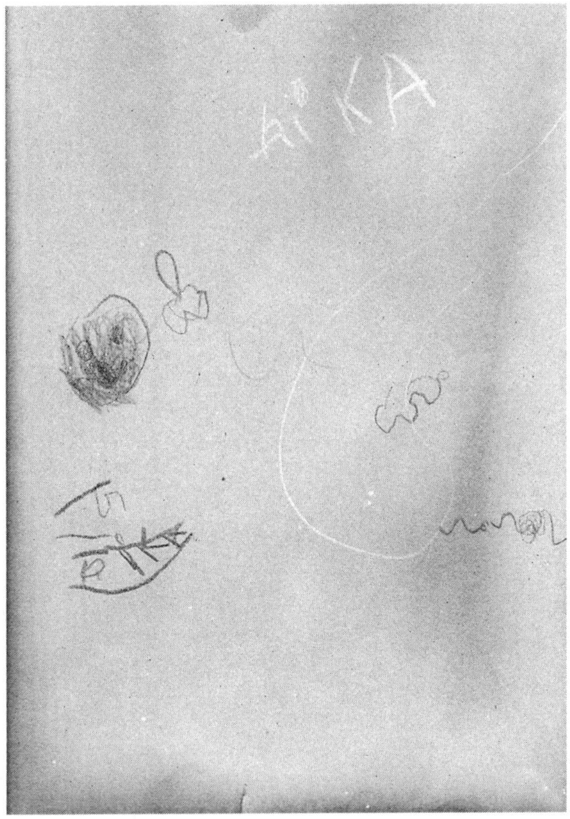

In a collaborative study of Rika's drawing, educators noticed lines that curve and squiggle and saw things that they recognized: an insect, a flower, a happy face, and a few other items. They noticed that she covers the whole page and she seems to have intentionally connected the different aspects of her drawing together. The lines and squiggles seem to represent movement. The journey of the insect perhaps? Do those objects represent things the insect encounters on his path? We believe there is a story unfolding here where Rika uses actions (verbs) and objects (nouns) to communicate what she knows.

Studying children's drawings in this way can help educators exercise their own observational skills and practice making meaning. It can help educators see competence in children and expand their ideas about the value of drawings. Try using these questions as one way to study children's drawings together.

Find words that you think best describe marks, such as smooth, curved, twisted, etc.

Where do you see the child experimenting with different pressure to make light or heavy marks?

Are there representations that you recognize?

What do you notice about the child's use of space? Did they stay in one corner? Did they use the whole page?

How would the child have moved their body (tiny finger movements, whole arm . . .)?

Are there any details that might give clues about what the child might have been thinking or feeling?

What questions does this drawing conjure up for you?

The children themselves can be the most important partners in thinking and studying their drawings. With some thoughtful conversation, they can help reveal their own theories and ideas, which can lead to new questions and new considerations. Here is an example of how studying children's drawings led to a long-term study in a preschool classroom.

In Jen and Lindsay's preschool class, the children were enthralled with the Magic Tree House book series. In each book, main characters Jack and Annie go on adventures where they encounter some sort of a problem. Jen and Lindsay decided to invite the children to consider what they would do if they were faced with a problem similar to one in the day's book, and draw out their ideas. The children's drawings were imaginative and interesting, and they enjoyed using pencil and paper to share their ideas. Jen and Lindsay made a point of pulling out a new challenge from the Jack and Annie books every week for the children to draw. It soon became obvious to Jen and Lindsay that these beautiful drawings revealed a great deal about the children's personality and understanding. They wanted to learn more and so they met with each child and asked them to talk about the ideas and theories in their drawings.

In this example, Jen and Lindsay asked the children, "How would you help animals cross a river?" They talked with the children and wrote down what they said. Then Jen and Lindsay studied the documentation together and came up with their own questions and theories about the children's understanding and thinking.

Abdullah offered that he would "bring the wind to blow the water away."

Abdullah understands that the wind is powerful.

Does he believe that he can summon the wind himself?

Where does he think the water will go?

Ivy said she would "Give him water wings."

This is a resourceful solution. Water wings are helpful to children who are learning to swim.

Is Ivy showing an understanding that you can do things alone if you have the right tools?

Vittoria's idea is that they should "lift them over." Vittoria includes herself in the solution. Her drawing shows her mom and dad working together to help.

There are ideas of collective strength and altruism here.

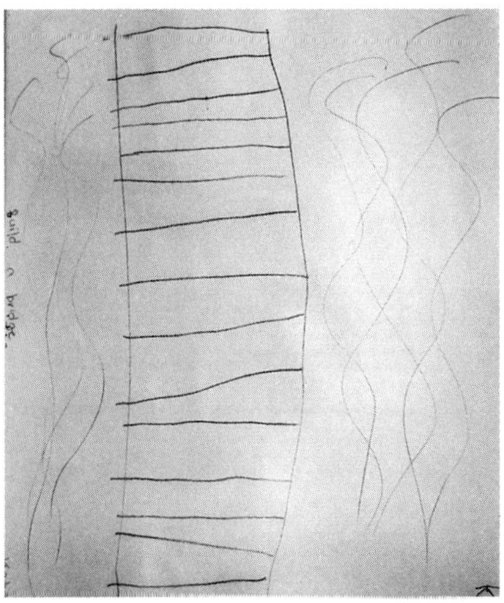

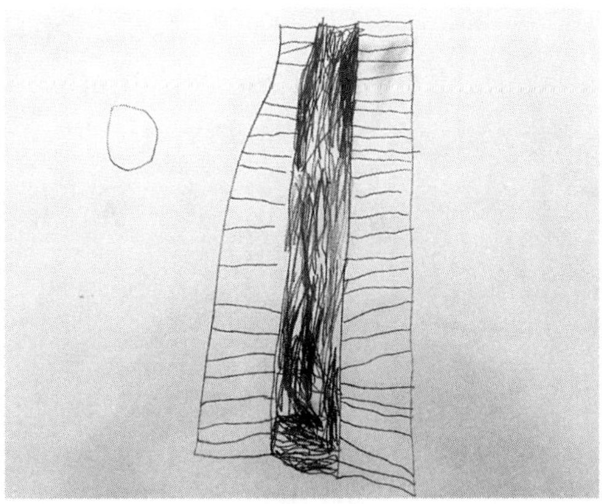

Several children said they would "build a bridge" or "use a bridge."

This showed that there was common understanding among the children that a bridge could be a useful solution.

This could have been the end of the experience, but the educators saw potential here and thought about how this could an opportunity for the children to test their theories in real life. Jen and Lindsay met with all of the children, and through a thoughtful process of sharing, questioning, listening, and considering, the class decided to test out two of the children's ideas together. This created the catalyst for a long-term study on bridge building.

Engaging in conversations with children about their drawings can shed light on children's thinking and can sometimes reveal new opportunities. In this case, there was a clear path that emerged.

1. The educators offered the children a specific provocation to draw.
2. The educators invited the children to talk about their drawing.
3. The educators captured in writing what the children said.
4. The educators studied their documentation and developed their own theories and questions.
5. The educators invited the children to share their drawings and ideas with each other.
6. The educators facilitated a conversation with the children to help them choose an idea to work with.

Once Jen and Lindsay would have been content with simply posting the children's beautiful drawings on a bulletin board. However, multiple experiences working alongside a pedagogical leader helped them become familiar with the process of thinking with children's drawings. The mentoring and support that they had received over the years helped them become pedagogical leaders for each other.

Studying Educator Writing Together

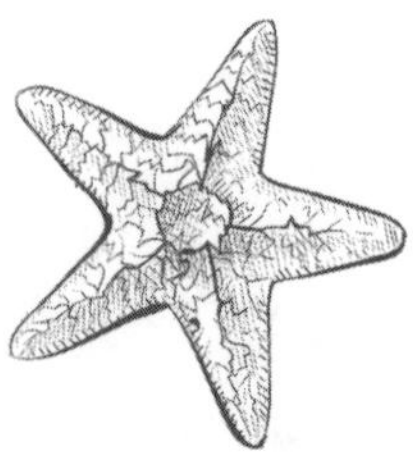

In classrooms all across North America, there is a growing expectation that we take up the practice of documentation in different ways. While photographs and samples of children's work can be valuable sources for study and reflection, it is through writing that educators and pedagogical leaders can document, reflect on, and share their own thoughts and questions. Rather than striving for polished pieces of writing that focus on assessing children, we are interested in how educators can learn how to use documentation to help them learn more about themselves and the impact of their practice.

In actual fact, what we write about someone else says more about us than the person we are writing about. It reveals the things that are most relevant to us in that moment. It provides glimpses into what we value. It sheds light on what we are thinking about, what we know about a topic, what we care about, what we believe, and what we think is important. Our writing can be a mirror that offers insights into the nuances of our own thinking and therefore can be one of the most valuable professional learning tools at our disposal.

Studying educator writing is perhaps one of the more challenging practices to establish. It requires a deep trust and an understanding that documentation is not meant to be private. Pedagogical leaders can help educators understand that their writing doesn't have to be a polished finished product or a declaration of what they know. It can be something that starts a conversation, ignites an idea, engages others, or leaves a trail of thinking to look back on. The Layered Voices exercise we offered previously is one way pedagogical leaders can engage educators in thinking along with each other's writing. Here we offer you a structure where educators and pedagogical leaders can study their own writing.

Plan: Choose a time and a place to write. This might seem obvious, but setting specific parameters will help you make it a priority in your day. It doesn't need to take a long time. When you have a structure to work with, even five minutes a day can be all you need. It is useful if you have several pieces of writing to look at rather than just one. Plan to have five or six pieces before you go back and study them.

Prepare: Ensure you have the necessary tools. Whether you choose to write the old-fashioned way with pen and paper or with technology, having what you need with you will ensure that you don't waste valuable writing time searching for something.

Write: Choose one of these phrases to get you started and write. Just write. Don't worry about spelling or being poetic or saying the wrong thing. Let your thoughts flow onto the paper (or screen).

- Something that touched my heart today . . .
- Something that worried me today . . .
- Something I did today that I question . . .
- Something I saw that delighted me . . .

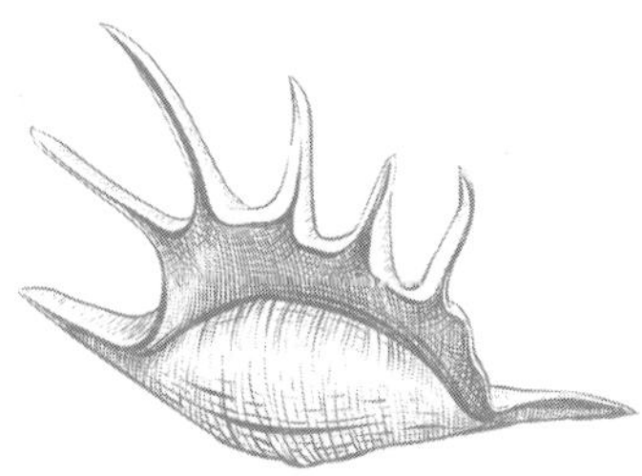

- Something I thought about when I watched the children interact with each other . . .
- Something I felt about my work today . . .
- Something I noticed in myself today . . .
- Something I noticed in the children today . . .

Reflect: Reflect on what you wrote and have a conversation about it. Here is where you can bring in others to help you unpack the ideas revealed through your writing. While the focus of the conversation is your writing, the conversations can help others in the group make connections with their own practice.

- Consider some of the words you use to describe your experiences, and study them together.
- What are the words that stand out to you or for others? These might be repeated words or strong words.
- What do they reveal to you about how you might have been thinking or feeling at the time?
- Have a conversation about the meaning of some of these words. Share your interpretations. How does the choice of one word over another affect how you come to think about your work?
- What does your writing reveal about what is capturing your attention?
- As you read through different entries, do you see common threads or themes?
- Are some children showing up in your writing more than others?
- What different values do you think might be at play here?

While anyone can use and add to this structure, many educators find it helpful to have a pedagogical leader act as a facilitator. Studying your own writing with others requires trust and vulnerability. Pedagogical leaders can create a safe space to work through this process where educators don't have to see their writing as right or wrong or good or bad but as a valuable tool that provides insight into their own thinking and practice.

As educators move through this process over and over, sharing their own work and engaging with the work of others, they develop a greater awareness of themselves and the role that documentation plays in professional learning.

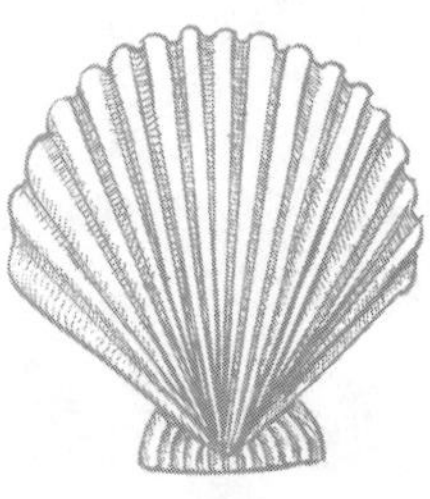

PEDAGOGICAL LEADERS SUPPORT EDUCATORS IN CREATING INDIVIDUAL LEARNING PLANS

Now consider . . .

How do you decide what you want to learn more about?

What are the values or goals that guide your decisions on learning?

What emotions bubble up for you when you think of performance management, reviews, appraisals, and evaluations? Was there a time in your career when you had to write a performance evaluation for staff or when you were on the receiving end of the review? We have been on both ends of the review. In many cases they would happen once a year, often connected to an annual salary increase. Traditionally, performance reviews or evaluations focus on the areas where educators need to develop stronger skills and in many cases include goal setting for the year ahead. Although intended to support employee growth, the annual review often does just the opposite. It is often an anxious time when educators nervously wait to hear how their supervisor views their performance and what weaknesses they need to work on. There is a real tug of war between accountability and development. But over the years we have seen a shift from accountability to learning. This has led our organizations to develop structures that support the development of individual professional learning plans. The learning plans, unlike the reviews, are developed by educators, take a strengths-based approach, and parallel the kind of practice we want educators to take up in the classroom. If we believe that children deserve to engage in learning opportunities that build on their strengths and are based on their interests, our practices with educators should hold these same values. We believe that growing children deserve growing educators, and as such our organizations have had a long-standing commitment to professional learning. Each year we offer a wide array of internal professional development, engage in book studies and classroom research, and seek out external opportunities that align with our organizations' pedagogical goals. Our process now engages educators in creating their own individual learning goals, considering what they are curious to learn and how these curiosities connect with the overall goals of the organization. The role of the pedagogical leader is to engage in the process alongside the educators. Listen to the story of how Christine, a pedagogical leader, engages in the process alongside an educator who is new to the organization.

Reiko, an educator who has been in the field for several years, had just joined the preschool team and was excited to be part of this new program.

The program was known in the community for innovative approaches and a strong commitment to learning. The first few months she was busy getting to know the children, families, routines, and schedules. There were a few staff meetings, and she was grateful for the planning time each week as well as meetings with Christine to orient herself to the program's philosophy, goals, and practices. Christine had explained that once Reiko was settled, they would meet together to consider her learning goals for the year ahead. In their first meeting, Christine offered Reiko the template that she would be using to outline her goals but wanted first to talk a little more about the pedagogical goals and values of the program. Christine explained that the goals and values could act as a compass and provide some direction for the learning path Reiko wanted to take up. She offered Reiko questions to reflect on and encouraged her to write her thoughts and bring them to their next meeting.

> What kinds of professional learning opportunities have you been drawn to in the past?
>
> How have these affected your practice?
>
> What have been the major shifts in learning for you in the past few years?

Pause and Reflect

What learning opportunities have had the greatest impact on you as an educator?

What shifts in your practice have you noticed?

When they met again the following week, Christine could see how the questions had helped Reiko reveal how she learns best and the kinds of experiences and resources that have had the greatest influence on her work as an educator. Christine then invited her to consider:

> What goals and values of the program really resonate with you as an educator?
>
> What strengths do you notice in your practice that align with these goals?
>
> What are you curious to learn more about?

Christine could see that Reiko was gaining a deeper understanding of the values of the organization and that she was able to see how they lived within the classroom and the program as a whole. She encouraged Reiko to take some time before their next meeting to consider what learning goals she wanted to set for herself in the coming year. After two weeks passed, Christine and Reiko met again. With notes in hand, Reiko talked about how she felt that she had some understanding of documentation but felt she wanted to learn more about how she could use her notes and documentation to help her gain a deeper understanding of the children. She also noted that she had a keen interest in developing an antibias approach in her work with children. She knew this was an important focus for the program and was eager to find ways to bring it to her classroom practice. Both of Reiko's goals clearly aligned with the program's values and goals, and Christine could see Reiko's genuine excitement.

Reiko had created a clear vision for herself, and once she was able to articulate her goals, Christine asked Reiko to consider a plan for her path forward in acting on the goals.

What workshops, networks, or discussion groups will I join?

What is happening in the community that I might tap into?

What books, resources, podcasts, webinars, or articles might I access?

What are the strengths of my team that may support my goals?

What timeline will I set for myself for these goals?

Reiko took the time to do some research and seek out possible resources and opportunities to work toward her goals. In the coming months Reiko started her learning path, taking part in workshops and webinars and reading on her own. In conversations in the staff room, Reiko connected with others in the program who had similar goals, and together they began to share resources. After a few months had passed, Christine set a meeting with Reiko to reflect on her goals with her. Together they discussed Reiko's progress in working toward her learning plan. Christine used the following questions to guide their dialogue.

How is your learning affecting your daily practice?

What have you learned about yourself?

What have you learned about others?

What are you curious to learn more about now?

How might you share with others what you have discovered?

At the end of the meeting Reiko was able to identify ways her learning was influencing her work in the classroom as well as her relationships with the team. These meetings took place every few months, with each one evolving Reiko's learning goals and keeping her moving forward.

In the classroom the role of the educator is to create a space where children are engaged, where they are able to express their ideas, explore their curiosities, and feel valued for who they are. The role of the educator is not to "teach" children but rather to set a space where learning can happen. The same is true for pedagogical leaders. Pedagogical leaders understand that educators deserve to explore their own ideas and feel engaged in learning. Each of us has to own the responsibility for our own learning, and the role of the pedagogical leader is to hold a space for learning to happen and support the process. By the same token, programs and organizations that can name their values and goals provide a compass to support educators in their learning paths. In this way programs see movement. Learning is a social process with children and with adults.

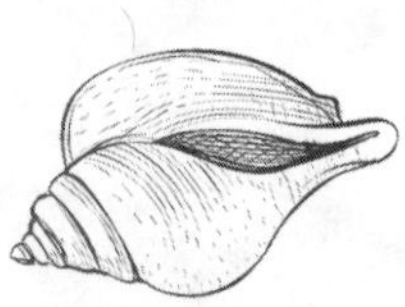

"Setting learning goals provides me with a framework from which I can design my own learning plan. Goals keep me accountable to my own growth and progression. When I am thinking about learning goals, I try to think of them in broad terms, like what areas can I/should I focus on that would support me in becoming the best mentor/best educator/best human I can be? When I look at it this way, my goals are passion driven and I am naturally invested in becoming the best version of myself in the most authentic way."

Shelley, educator

Exploring Pedagogical Practice: Creating Professional Learning Goals

Growing children deserve growing educators. An important part of our learning is to articulate a vision and goals for ourselves stemming from our curiosity and to generate new ideas we want to explore in our own professional learning journey. Using your program's values, goals, or pedagogical focuses, invite educators to consider one or two professional learning goals for themselves.

The following questions can help educators consider how they learn best, refine their understanding of the program's learning goals, and provide a baseline to create their individual learning plan.

1. Take some time to reflect and consider:

What kinds of professional learning opportunities have you been drawn to in the past?

How have these affected your practice?

What major shifts in learning have you experienced in the past few years?

Which program goals and values resonate with you as an educator?

What strengths do you notice in your practice that align with these goals?

What are you curious to learn more about?

After you have had a chance to consider these questions, write one or two professional learning goals for yourself.

2. Consider the kinds of resources and supports that can help you achieve your goals:

What workshops, networks, or discussion groups will I join?

What is happening in the community that I might tap into?

What books, resources, podcasts, webinars, or articles might I access?

What are the strengths of my team that may support my goals?

What timeline will I set for myself for these goals?

3. After a few months of working through your learning plan, consider:

How is your learning affecting your daily practice?

What have you learned about yourself?

What have you learned about others?

What are you curious to learn more about now?

How might you share with others what you have discovered?

www.redleafpress.org/crp/d-11.pdf

PEDAGOGICAL LEADERS UNDERSTAND THE MOST POWERFUL LEARNING HAPPENS SIDE BY SIDE

Now consider . . .

What learning moments in the classroom have been the most powerful for you?

What intentional practices do you consider when working side by side with educators?

As we have mentioned several times throughout this book, we believe that questions drive our practice, not answers. In fact, our hope is always that questions engage our curiosities, and as we learn more, new questions arise. When pedagogical leaders are curious alongside educators, they become co-learners.

We can recall in our early days of practice as leaders that there was a feeling of responsibility to "teach" not only children but also the educators we worked with. If we noticed something in the classroom that we felt wasn't working, we would offer suggestions or strategies to change it, or we would role model how to be alongside children. We have learned that although our intentions were good, our practice was not growing capacity in educators, and that role modeling alone does not work. When pedagogical leaders and educators talk about why they do what they do, practice shifts and becomes more intentional.

Rosa, a young early childhood educator in a preschool classroom, was struggling with two very spirited boys. She often felt the two had a love-hate relationship. Each day they waited for the other to arrive and would begin playing in the block area of the classroom. Although Justin, the smaller of the two, loved to share his ideas and build on the play that happened the previous day, he typically followed Evan's lead. The play would begin with joyful laughter and engagement but often shifted to raised voices and aggressive behavior when Justin wanted to try something different. Worried about the children hurting each other, Rosa often stopped the play and suggested the boys separate if they were not able to play together without fighting. This often resulted in Justin giving up his ideas and following Evan. Rosa felt bad for Justin but was at a loss. Brian, the program's pedagogical leader, spent a morning in the preschool room and also noticed the play dynamic. Without saying a word, he placed himself near the play, sitting close to Justin. The play once again started with excitement and quickly shifted as the boys raised their voices at each other. Brian moved in a little closer to Justin, listening to their discussion. As Justin was about to give in to Evan, Brian moved in closer still and placed his hand on Justin's back. As Rosa watched, she could see a shift in Justin. He stood a little taller and became more assertive with his ideas. For what felt like the first time, Evan stood back and agreed to change the course of play. The play began again, this time with renewed energy and engagement.

Later that day, Brian connected with Rosa to debrief the morning observations. Initially she thought perhaps the boys' play was different because Brian was male. When Brian shared his reflections and his intentions, though, she better understood what she had witnessed. Brian said he had also noticed the boys' relationship, and rather than stopping the play, he was curious about how he might lend his power to Justin. He had intentionally thought about where he should place himself near the play, and as the play began to heighten, he moved closer to Justin to offer him quiet support. He didn't need to say anything; his placement alone and his gentle support on Justin's back gave him confidence. A light bulb went off for Rosa, and her practice began to shift. She became more curious about when and how she placed herself in the classroom, noticing how her presence alone could influence children's play. In weeks and months ahead, Rosa and Brian studied this in the classroom together. As she tells this story now, she often talks about this small moment in a classroom so many years ago that in many ways shaped who she is as an educator and her understanding of her power in the classroom. Rosa's practice shifted, not because Brian had modeled a different way to be alongside children but because Brian shared why he did what he did and his thinking behind it, and together they became curious to learn more.

Pause and Reflect

How have the practices of others in the classroom shifted your practice?

How do you reflect with others about the intentional practices you take up in the classroom?

"To enter into a style of teaching which is based on questioning what we're doing and why, on listening to children, on thinking about how theory is translated into practice and how practice informs theory, is to enter into a way of working where professional development takes place day after day in the classroom."

Sonya Shoptaugh

The role of the pedagogical leader is to find a way to embed professional learning into everyday practice. For many years we have thought of professional learning as something that happens outside of the classroom, taking place in the evening or on a weekend after a long week of work. Pedagogical leaders understand that some of the most powerful learning experiences happen side by side with educators in the classroom.

Because we authors both started our practice in the classroom, when we moved into roles as supervisors and directors, we were eager to be the best leaders we could. For many years as we were finding our way, we used our time in the classroom for watching and evaluating educators' practices. In fact, in Ontario, our licensing system required this of us. We felt it was our job to observe educators in action and help them grow their practice by sharing what we noticed, both strengths and challenges. When our practice shifted from watching educators to watching children alongside educators, everything changed. This comes to life in this story about how Lisa, a pedagogical leader, takes up the idea of seeing children together alongside educators.

In her practice Lisa worked hard to carve out time each week to spend alongside educators in the classrooms and found ways to meet with classroom teams every couple of weeks. Mondays were her usual day to spend time in the toddler room, and the educators always welcomed the extra set of hands. The room was very busy, and Lisa noticed that the children spent a great deal of their morning disengaged. The children were dumping everything and throwing materials, and there were frequent struggles with children taking each other's things. It felt like chaos, and when one child cried, it seemed to spread. She could see why the educators were so thankful for her time in the room, but she knew that just managing behavior was not the role she wanted to play as the pedagogical leader, nor the one that educators wanted to play each day.

In her own observations she could see that the environment was affecting the children's interactions. The room seemed sparse, and much of the equipment had limited possibilities. She had been learning about schema play and how children naturally organize their experiences through repeated patterns of behavior in their play. These patterns are natural urges that are building blocks for the brain, and they help create the solid connections that are necessary for learning and development. Knowing this, Lisa began to wonder if the classroom environment was offering the complexity that children's brains require.

Lisa shared what she was learning about schema play and invited the educators to read more together. In their next meeting together, Lisa gathered a variety of loose parts and materials that provided possibilities for filling and dumping, connecting, rolling and spinning, and more, and asked the educators to bring similar materials. Together they collected balls, bowls, tubes, ramps, pegs, wheels, and a multitude of other loose parts. Placing all the materials on the floor, together they began to play. As they played Lisa asked them to consider:

What are you drawn to with the materials?

How can you use the materials in different ways?

As you are learning about materials, what new discoveries are you making?

After some time had passed in the play, they discussed these questions, and Lisa offered new questions to consider how they might be offered to the children.

What do you think the children might do with the materials?

How might we present these possibilities in the classroom?

What role do we want to play alongside the children?

The educators expressed their concerns with offering the materials to the children. Their days already felt filled with picking up after the children and policing play. They were concerned that the materials would invite more of these challenges, but they were willing to try it. They decided they would set up a space with the materials the next day and divide into two groups. One group would remain outside while another group was invited inside to play. Together they selected materials to set up in the classroom, and Lisa offered some questions they could study during the play.

How are the children using the materials?

What are we learning about the children in the play?

How do the children use the materials to engage each other and build relationships?

The next morning, Lisa joined them in the classroom to set up the experience and offered to engage in the play with the children so the educators could spend more time observing. She suggested taking photos and notes that they could look at together in their next meeting. They also discussed the role that they would each take up in the play. Jessica was going to take the role of the observer and documenter while Lisa and Sabrina would join the children on the floor. Lisa suggested they try not to ask questions or give directions to the children but rather describe and narrate the children's play and their ideas back to them.

As the team was preparing to decide which group of children would come inside, both educators suggested that Evan stay outside. During their discussion the previous day around how the children might use the materials, the team had expressed concern specifically around Evan. They had been struggling with him and mentioned that he was having a really difficult time engaging in play and was the first to throw things and take them from others. In hearing this, Lisa suggested that they invite Evan, and she would stay close with him as needed. All agreed, so they went outside to gather the children.

When the children entered the room, Lisa was on the floor with Sabrina, while Jessica sat to the side, camera and notebook in hand, ready to watch the play.

The children's eyes lit up as they moved closer to the experience. They quickly engaged with the materials. Lisa and Sabrina stayed close, working hard to avoid asking questions or giving direction to the children. It was difficult at first, but they began to notice how engaged the children were. It had already been twenty-five minutes of focused play. At one point, Evan was watching Joel spin a sparkling ball inside a plastic bowl. He seemed mesmerized by the color and the movement. Lisa was watching his gaze. Evan reached out for the bowl and ball, taking it from Joel. Joel tugged back and a conflict seemed imminent. Lisa calmly noticed, "Evan was watching you with the ball. He really likes your idea of spinning and wants to try your idea too." In just that moment, Joel released the bowl and passed it to Evan, who began spinning. Both Sabrina and Jessica took notice of this and expressed both their surprise and delight. The children played for more than forty-five minutes together, trying each other's ideas and exploring the materials.

When the team came together later that afternoon to debrief the experiences, they were excited to share their observations and excitement from the morning. Lisa offered more questions to guide their discussion.

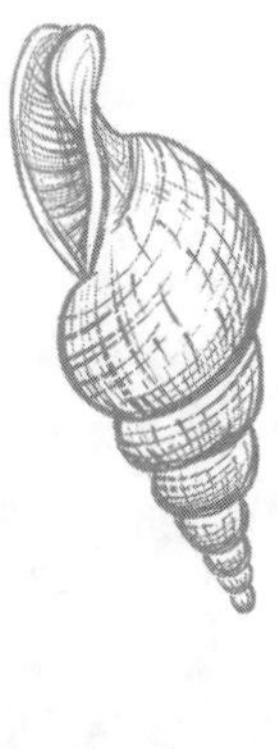

What really resonated with you as you watched the play?

How did the environment influence the play?

What did you notice about how the children used the materials to build relationships?

What words might you use to describe children's competence?

What role did the educators play in the experience?

What does this experience have you thinking about in your practice as you move forward?

Lisa's questions were inspired by the Thinking Lens® (see page 141) and helped the educators look closely at aspects of both their experience and the children's.

The educator team reflected on how the materials kept the children engaged for such a long time and discussed the role the educators had played in staying close and noticing and naming what they were seeing. They reflected on Evan in the play and wondered if many of his actions had more to do with the environment and their role in play than it actually had to do with him. It was a sobering moment for the team as they began to see more clearly that their interactions and the environment had a great deal to do with the managing and policing roles they had been playing. They were excited to think of new experiences they could offer children and wanted to engage their lens on schema play to be sure that the materials they were using provided the complexity the children's brains required.

Pedagogical leaders understand that their role is not to tell educators what to put in their classrooms or how to set up the environment but rather to offer questions and ways for educators to see for themselves the powerful role that materials play in engaging learning environments. When pedagogical leaders engage educators in the learning side by side, educators can see the power of engagement over compliance in their work with children.

> *"Side by sides offer opportunities for educators to lean in, observe, take notes, and then come together to reflect on these observations. Spending time thinking alongside a mentor, while really listening and noticing children's strengths and competencies, and then bring[ing] visibility to it. Working in collaboration invites multiple perspectives to really dig into the children's learning."*
>
> ~ *Tina, pedagogical leader*

Exploring Pedagogical Practice: Learning Side by Side with Educators in Practice

<table>
<tr><td>Plan a Team Meeting
Set aside time in a team meeting to explore new materials for the classroom. Invite educators to gather materials they are drawn to and believe children will be drawn to. Bring along some additional materials that you are interested in exploring as well.</td><td>Take time to explore the materials together and consider the following questions.
What are you drawn to with the materials?
How can you use the materials in different ways?
As you are learning about materials, what discoveries are you making?
After you have taken some time to really explore the materials, pause and consider:
What do you think the children might do with the materials?
How might we present these possibilities in the classroom?
What role do we want to play alongside the children?</td></tr>
<tr><td>Offer the Materials to the Children
Make a plan to offer the experience in the classroom. Consider together where the materials will be set up as well as who and how many children you want to engage. This is also a time to consider who will play with the children and who will observe.</td><td>When engaging in play:
Take up the role of listener. Watch the children play, and offer it back to them. The role is not to lead the play but rather to describe and narrate what you see. Help children see each other's ideas as they try out the materials.
Consider the following questions as you listen and watch the play:
How are the children using the materials?
What are we learning about the children in the play?
How do the children use the materials to engage each other and build relationships?</td></tr>
<tr><td>Debrief the Experience
Gather after the experience to have a conversation around everyone's observations. This is a good time to share photos, notes, or personal reflections.</td><td>In your debrief use these questions inspired by Thinking Lens® to guide the discussion.
What really resonated with you as you watched the play?
How did the environment influence the play?
What did you notice about how the children used the materials to build relationships?
What words might you use to describe the children's competence?
What role did the educators play in the experience?
What does this experience have you thinking about in your practice as you move forward?</td></tr>
</table>

PEDAGOGICAL LEADERS HAVE CLEAR PEDAGOGICAL FOCUSES TO ORIENT THEIR WORK

Now consider . . .

What kinds of things do you find get most of your attention during the day?

How do you decide where to spend time, energy, and money?

During the initial stages of the COVID-19 shutdown when most child care centers in Ontario were forced to close their doors, there were a handful across the province that opened up as emergency centers for essential workers, including some of our centers from London Bridge and Compass. This was of course a time of heightened concern, and stress levels were high for everyone. Daily announcements about rising cases and new information about how the virus was spreading infiltrated news and social media. A continuous stream of new child care regulations served as a daily reminder of the heightened responsibility educators had in keeping children safe. While additional measures were put into place to support wellness, like wearing personal protection equipment (PPE), doing prescreening health checks on children and their families prior to entering, isolating classrooms from each other, and constantly disinfecting, they actually caused added stress and anxiety. Even though the goal was to create safe, caring spaces for children, there was a palpable unintended narrative that focused more on illness than wellness.

Picking up on this, one of our pedagogical leaders offered the idea of intentionally focusing on the concept of wellness, rather than illness, to help orient them in the opening and operation of the emergency care sites. When parents and children were met at the door by an educator covered head to toe in full PPE, they began to ask themselves, "How do I bring wellness to this moment?" Simply asking this question affected the way educators interacted with nervous families and children. They were more aware of their own body language. They were joyful and reassuring, which helped put children, families, and themselves at greater ease. As the days and weeks passed, together the educators and pedagogical leader continued to focus on wellness. They shared different ideas about what wellness meant to them. They learned about and implemented mindfulness practices in their classrooms. They considered how wellness can live in moments of frustration and conflict as well as in times of joyfulness. They searched for places where wellness existed in the world and started to think more about the wellness of the earth and their relationship with the land around them. Using wellness as a pedagogical focus provided them with a specific way to think and move in their work. It helped them examine themselves, grow new understandings, and come up with questions that they hadn't considered before about what it actually means to be well. During this time of heightened pressure and responsibility, it could have been easy for these educators and their pedagogical leader to let the stress of the situation consume them. However, by drawing on the idea of wellness as a pedagogical focus, it enabled them to make intentional decisions about where to give their energies, and it helped them stay calm and attentive even during a global crisis.

Pedagogical focuses can offer us an intentional way to orient ourselves in our work. Like a compass they provide direction and can help guide how we spend time, money, energy, and resources. In any given day, pedagogical leaders and educators are faced with a multitude of decisions that can sometimes feel overwhelming. What issues or moments do you choose to give your attention to? What emerging new interest do you follow? What topics do you construct your conversations around? What kinds of professional learning do you offer or engage in?

Rather than laying out a specific road map for constructing a curriculum, pedagogical focuses provide you with conceptual ideas to consider as you move through your day. Your pedagogical focuses come from the things that are most important to you. They are linked closely to your values and are in response to the kind of culture you are trying to create.

In our province, *How Does Learning Happen? Ontario's Pedagogy for the Early Years* offers the ideas of belonging, engagement, expression, and well-being as foundations for learning (Ontario Public Service 2014). These foundations are born from a shared belief across our province that for learning to happen, children and adults both deserve to have opportunities to engage fully in the world, express ideas in different ways, and feel a sense of belonging and well-being while they do it. We think of these four foundations as pedagogical focuses. Rather than outlining a step-by-step process to ensure a specific outcome, they provide educators and pedagogical leaders a way to think about their daily practice, grow their understanding, and uncover the complexities that live within their work.

Consider the idea of *belonging*. When educators and pedagogical leaders focus their attention and thinking around this idea, they start to ask themselves questions like:

What does it mean to belong?

How do you know when you belong somewhere?

What kinds of things will we see that show us children feel like they belong in our classroom?

How do we know when someone doesn't feel like they belong?

Who does our classroom, center, or organization make feel welcome, and who is excluded?

How do we create space where people with diverse backgrounds and experiences can feel like they belong?

How do we consider the nonhumans that we share the earth with in our ideas of belonging?

These kinds of questions can provide direction and give purpose to our work. They help guide how we use our time and how we make decisions. Both our organizations, London Bridge and Compass, use these foundational concepts offered by our province as pedagogical focuses. We weave the ideas of belonging, engagement, expression, and wellness together with the four goals of antibias education—identity, diversity, fairness, and justice—and use them to think about our relationship with each other and the earth. Sometimes educators and pedagogical leaders choose to think about and move with a particular pedagogical focus intensely over a period of time, such as wellness in the previous story. Other times, they might merge them together or draw on a pedagogical focus that is inspired by an encounter or a particular situation. In any case, our pedagogical focuses are always there to act as a guidepost for our thinking, learning, and decision-making.

> *"I view our pedagogical focuses as building blocks that we get to play with in our creations. Our pedagogical focuses remain vague because I believe that they are supposed to be expansive. They are supposed to leave space for innovation and newness. They are supposed to grow with us in our journey. They are not instructional protocols to follow, but they are a wonderful companion in decision-making."*
>
> *Renee, pedagogical leader*

Pedagogical focuses can come from different places. Sometimes they are provided for you in provincial or state curriculum frameworks such as *How Does Learning Happen? Ontario's Pedagogy for the Early Years* (Ontario Public Service 2014). Other times they can come from a center or organization's values and vision, such as desire to create inclusive, diverse, and equitable learning environments. Wherever they come from, these are the overarching ideas that matter most to you and help guide how you move in your practice.

In our work, we have found that our pedagogical focuses have grown in response to the times we live in and the state of the world around us. Children, like all of us, are affected by issues of inequity and systemic racism and the impact of human behavior on the planet. When we can focus our pedagogies around ideas that recognize and counter these things, like belonging, diversity, and connection to the land, we can help inspire much-needed change.

Exploring Your Own Practice: Thinking about Your Pedagogical Focuses

Take some time to think with your colleagues about the overarching ideas that guide your practice and decision-making. Consider together:

Where do these ideas come from?

In what ways are they important to you?

How do they align with your program or organizational values?

What pedagogical focuses are offered to you in your provincial or state early learning framework?

What might you add to that list based on what you see happening in the world and the kind of community you want to build?

Making decisions around the foundational ideas that guide your teaching practice is a political act. This is not something that most early childhood educators often think about in their work. However, the reality is that educational systems are built around political structures. Values are taught through education: choices are made, and particular histories are shared and considered while others are intentionally left out. It is through education that a particular type of citizen is molded and prepared for society. The question "What is education for?" is a political question that is rooted in a society's agenda for its children. The choices we make as educators about what to teach, how to teach, and how to think about teaching have impact.

Consider the words of teacher and activist Betsy Warner in her essay "Education Is Political":

> In the curriculum and in the choices we make about what to teach and how to teach it, education is political. And, for the most part, our country's curriculum is white. Our nation's curriculum primarily presents people of European descent, and specifically men, as the movers and shakers in history, math, science, literature, art, and music (2017).

Pause and Reflect

Who are the people who influence how you approach your teaching practice?

How are the decisions you make about what and how to teach political?

Murray Sinclair of Manitoba is a former member of the Canadian Senate and is a First Nations lawyer who served as chair of the Indian Residential Schools Truth and Reconciliation Commission of Canada (TRC) from 2009 to 2015. The TRC published ninety-four calls to action urging all levels of government to work together to change policies and programs to repair the harm caused by Indian residential schools across Canada. During one of his lectures on the TRC, Senator Sinclair talked about the sacred responsibility that educators have to ensure that all children are able to think about certain key questions all throughout their education, including *where do I come from?, where am I going?, why am I here?,* and *who am I?* He suggested that educational systems matter and should be designed to help children find these answers.

Pause and Reflect

How do these questions differ from the kinds of questions that have historically driven education in Canada and the United States?

How does this make you think about your sacred responsibilities to children?

It can be easy to dismiss the idea that early childhood education is political. However, the reality is that the decisions that we make in our classrooms and organizations are political. Each time we make the decision to give time and energy to one idea over another, we are making a political choice that has an impact on those around us. Working with intentional pedagogical focuses is one way that teachers and pedagogical leaders can acknowledge and embrace the political choices that they are making in classrooms and organizations every day.

RECAPPING THE ROLE OF THE PEDAGOGICAL LEADER TO SUPPORT LEARNING IN MULTIPLE WAYS

Pedagogical leaders . . .

- See the importance of engaging educators as active participants in their own learning.
- Explore ways that educators learn best.
- Understand that questions drive practice, not answers.
- See professional learning as a way to develop our profession.
- Use a pedagogical focus to guide practice and thinking.
- Build pedagogical practice around ideas that are important for the world we live in today.
- Make intentional decisions about the kinds of professional learning they invest in.
- Explore pedagogies and frameworks to understand foundations for learning.
- Support a pedagogical approach to hiring, using questions to uncover educators' natural dispositions.
- Intentionally nurture dispositions that support the overall culture the program is trying to grow.
- Understand that learning takes time and is ever growing and evolving.
- Help uncover, understand, and disrupt some of the narratives that influence educator thinking.
- Engage educators in the practice of reflecting on and revisiting ideas over time.
- Embrace multiple perspectives and value the differences each person brings to their practice.

- Use documentation as a source of collaborative study and reflection.
- Create opportunities and structures for educators to study photos, stories, children's work, and words.
- Invite educators to reflect on their own writing.
- Use structures to evolve practice and deepen thinking.
- Support educators to create professional learning plans that connect to their strengths and curiosities.
- Take time to revisit and evolve learning plans over time.
- Understand that the most powerful professional learning happens side by side with educators in the classroom.
- Engage educators in exploring materials that they offer children.

Moving an Elephant: Some Final Thoughts

Whether you are a leader in a small single-site child care program or part of a much larger multisite organization, whether you are employed in non-profit or commercial care, this work requires an unwavering commitment to pedagogy. It asks that we think critically about how we spend time and use resources and that we give attention to the values we are trying to grow in our programs.

Strong desire alone does not effect change. For reflective practice to happen, there needs to be a commitment behind it. It requires organizations to make a conscious investment of time, energy, and, yes, dollars. Throughout this book we have offered you a wide variety of structures to get you on your way, but the reality is, for these or any other structures to be useful, you must think critically with them, use them in appropriate contexts, play around with them, and see them evolve. It is not always easy, but we have witnessed firsthand in our own work the impact that this kind of commitment can have on an organization's culture.

The principles and structures we have offered in this book have been born out of our own organizations' evolution and our experiences as pedagogical leaders. Over the years London Bridge and Compass, our two equally large yet very different organizations, have been learning from and with each other in our own attempt (to borrow our earlier metaphor) to move an elephant. While neither is without its own problems and challenges, both London Bridge and Compass have committed to putting the kinds of organizational structures in place that enable us to support and grow our reflective culture and pedagogical practices.

As we continue our journey in this work, we are constantly reminded of our own uncertainty. Each day we stitch and weave and attempt to untangle the many narratives we have inherited about what it means to be a leader in the field of early childhood. We recognize that if we are to reimagine our work in today's changing world, we need to unlearn and liberate ourselves from the various scripts that have bound us to a particular way of being. We

need to resist passing down a reproduction of the past and learn to engage in a different kind of relationship with each other and the world around us.

As pedagogical leaders we know that we cannot do this work alone. We need others to walk alongside us. We need our own mentors to guide us on our journey. In writing this book we are reminded of the many skilled, gracious people who have held us up and pushed us along our own paths. We are forever grateful for the genuine interest and curiosity they took in our work. For seeing the possibility and potential of what we were doing before we did. For insisting that we write and share our stories with others. For relentlessly questioning us in ways that helped us to fill out our own thinking. For steering us to resources and connecting us to other people who share our passions for this work.

For us, pedagogical leadership is not about rank or status. It is not about teaching others what to do or how to think, and it is most assuredly not about ensuring quality. Pedagogical leadership is about creating conditions for relationships to flourish. It is about nurturing a very particular kind of culture where connections are formed between the kind of work we do and the kind of world we want to live in.

We are humbled to have each of you take this journey alongside us through the stories and experiences we have shared in this book. Our hope for you is to find pedagogical leaders in your lives who can help you grow and develop. In the words of our mentors, "Look in front of you, look to those who have offered you mentorship, and look behind you, as these are the people who will look to you."

References

Adams, Marilee, and Marshall Goldsmith. 2016. *Change Your Questions, Change Your Life: 12 Powerful Tools for Leadership, Coaching, and Life*. 3rd ed. Oakland, CA: Berrett-Koehler Publishers.

Buscaglia, Leo. 1983. *Living Loving and Learning*. Ballantine Books.

Carter, Margie, Luz Maria Casio, and Deb Curtis. 2021 *The Visionary Director: A Handbook for Dreaming, Organizing, and Improvising in Your Center*. 3rd ed. St. Paul, MN: Redleaf Press.

Carter, Karen, Chris Cotton, and Kirsten Hill. 2009. "Network Facilitation: The Power of Protocols." National College for School Leadership, UK.

Coughlin, Anne Marie, and Lorrie Baird. 2013. "Pedagogical Leadership." In *Think, Feel, Act,* compiled by The Ministry of Education, 16–20. Canada: Ontario. https://files.ontario.ca/edu-think-feel-act-lessons-from-research-about-young-children-en-2021-01-29.pdf.

City of Ottawa and City for All Women Initiative (CAWI). 2015. *Equity and Inclusion Lens Handbook*. 2nd ed. https://documents.ottawa.ca/sites/documents/files/ei_lens_hb_en.pdf.

Covey, Stephen. 1989. *The Seven Habits of Highly Effective People: Restoring the Character Ethic*. New York: Simon and Schuster.

Curtis, Deb, and Margie Carter. 2013. *The Art of Awareness: How Observation Can Transform Your Teaching*. 2nd ed. St. Paul, MN: Redleaf Press.

——. 2017. *Learning Together with Young Children: A Curriculum Framework for Reflective Teachers*. 2nd ed. St. Paul, MN: Redleaf Press.

Curtis, Deb, Margie Carter, Debbie Lebo, and Wendy C. M. Cividanes. 2013. *Reflecting in Communities of Practice: A Workbook for Early Childhood Educators*. St. Paul, MN: Redleaf Press.

Dimensions of Pedagogical Leadership in Early Childhood Education and Care. n.d. Elina Fonsén University of Tampere Finland. https://Ilrfec.org/Wp-Content/Uploads/Sites/67/2014/01/art_10Fonsen.Pdf.

Drummond, Tom. n.d. "Enterprise Talk." https://tomdrummond.com/leading-and-caring-for-children/enterprise-talk.

Friedman, Susan, and Alissa Mwenelupembe. 2020. *Each and Every Child: Using an Equity Lens When Teaching in Preschool*. The National Association for the Education of Young Children.

Harper, Gary. 2004. *The Joy of Conflict Resolution*. New Society Publishers.

Heikka, Johanna, and Manjula Waniganayake. 2011. "Pedagogical Leadership from a Distributed Perspective within the Context of Early Childhood Education," *International Journal of Leadership in Education* 14 (4): 499–512, doi:10.1080/13603124.2011.577909.

Katz, Lilian. 1979. Helping Others Learn to Teach: Some Principles and Techniques for Inservice Educators. Urbana, IL: ERIC Clearinghouse on Childhood Education.

Kimmerer, Robin Wall. 2015. *Braiding Sweetgrass: Indigenous Wisdom, Scientific Knowledge, and the Teachings of Plants*. Minneapolis, MN: Milkweed Editions.

Male, Trevor, and Ioanna Palaiologou. 2011. "Learning-Centred Leadership or Pedagogical Leadership? An Alternative Approach to Leadership in Education Contexts." *International Journal of Leadership in Education*. 15. 10.1080/13603124.2011.617839.

Maxwell, John. 2013. *5 Levels of Leadership: Proven Steps to Maximize Your Potential*. Center Street.

Macneill, Neil, Robert F. Cavanagh, and Steffan Silcox. 2005. "Pedagogic Leadership: Refocusing on Learning and Teaching." *International Electronic Journal for Leadership in Learning* 9 (2). https://eric.ed.gov/?id=EJ985373.

Moss, P., 2019. *Alternative Narratives in Early Childhood: An Introduction for Students and Practitioners*. Abingdon: Routledge.

National Association for the Education of Young Children (NAEYC). 2019. Advancing Equity in Early Childhood Education Position Statement.

Ontario Public Service. 2014. *How Does Learning Happen? Ontario's Pedagogy for the Early Years*. www.edu.gov.on.ca/childcare/howlearninghappens.pdf.

Pelo, Ann, and Margie Carter. 2018. *From Teaching to Thinking: A Pedagogy for Reimagining Our Work*. Lincoln, NE: Exchange Press.

Rinaldi, Carlina. 2005. *In Dialogue with Reggio Emilia*. London: Routledge Farmer.

School Reform Initiative. "Protocols." www.schoolreforminitiative.org/protocols.

Shillingstad Saundra L., Sheryl McGlamery, Barbara Davis, and Carol Gilles. 2014. "Navigating the Roles of Leadership: Mentors' Perspectives on Teacher Leadership." Paper presented at the conference of the Annual Meeting of the Association of Teacher Educators, St. Louis, MO, February 15–18.

Shoptaugh, Sonya, and S. Miller. 2004. "Reflections on a Journey of Inspiration: Teacher Change in Public Education." In *Next Steps toward Teaching the Reggio Way*, J. Hendrick, ed. Upper Saddle, NJ: Pearson Education.

Truth and Reconciliation Commission of Canada. "Our Mandate." www.trc.ca/about-us/our-mandate.html.

Warner, Betsy. 2017. "Education Is Political."

Zinsser, Katherine M., and Timothy W. Curby. n.d. Understanding Preschool Teachers' Emotional Support as a Function of Center Climate. https://doi.org/10.1177/2158244014560728.

Index